I0842911

Cognitive Behavioral Therapy

The 10 steps CBT Workbook with Techniques for Retraining Your Brain Made Simple. For Managing Anxiety, Depression, Anger, Panic and Intrusive Thoughts

© Copyright 2019 - All rights reserved.

The content contained within this book may not be reproduced, duplicated, or transmitted without direct written permission from the author or the publisher.

Under no circumstances will any blame or legal responsibility be held against the publisher, or author, for any damages, reparation, or monetary loss due to the information contained within this book, either directly or indirectly.

Legal Notice:

This book is copyright protected. It is only for personal use. You cannot amend, distribute, sell, use, quote or paraphrase any part, or the content within this book, without the consent of the author or publisher.

Disclaimer Notice:

Please note the information contained within this document is for educational and entertainment purposes only. All effort has been executed to present accurate, up to date, reliable, complete information. No warranties of any kind are declared or implied. Readers acknowledge that the author is not engaging in the rendering of legal, financial, medical, or professional advice. The content within this book has been derived from various sources. Please consult a licensed professional before attempting any techniques outlined in this book.

Table of Contents

Introduction

Congratulations on downloading *Cognitive Behavior Therapy* and thank you for doing so.

The secret to cognitive behavioral therapy is in the name-it is therapy that focuses on "cognition" and "behavior." This chapter will break down exactly what that means and contextualize CBT in terms of other therapeutic interventions. This will be helpful even if you don't have any previous knowledge or experience of therapy-you have an idea of what therapy should look like, even if only from TV, and it is useful to differentiate CBT from that conception.

"Cognitive therapies" treat behavior as mediated by thoughts. What you think determines what you do. Someone who is depressed has conscious thoughts that are negative and pessimistic these thoughts are possible to change. Early in the development of CBT, research was finding that people who had a "negative explanatory style" were more at risk for depression. That is, people who see the worst in situations or always look for a pessimistic read on a situation are more likely to become depressed. Cognitive therapy works to change the way you interpret and think about situations in order to improve the way you feel. All cognitive therapies, including CBT, emphasize education and learning new skills that can be used to change your own mind.

This book will cover the whole range of cognitive behavioral therapy. We will have examples of cognitive restructuring, coping skills, and problem solving. The goal is to help you learn to feel better in as many ways as possible. The goal is to help you find an approach that works for you. In order to do that, explore a wide variety of interventions and learn different skills. You will then be able to put them together in your own life.

There are plenty of books on this subject on the market, thanks again for choosing this one! Every effort was made to ensure it is full of as much useful information as possible, please enjoy!

Chapter 1: Identifying the Problem

As we get older, life throws at us some unexpected deals. In some cases, these raw deals can cause us mental disorders such as anxiety, depression, panic attacks, and anger, among others. Growing up, we are taught about life, but these lessons do not cover every aspect of it. Therefore, we find ourselves in situations beyond our current understanding. These situations can make us be anxious or worse, depressed.

Interestingly, most of our mental disorders arise not because of the situation we are in but because of our interpretation. We tend to interpret events and situations subjectively, meaning that our judgment s are normally biased. For instance, if you grew up in an environment where every mistake was punishable, and there was no forgiveness, you might assume that life is punishing. In fact, the thought of making a mistake can make you anxious and unable to do the things you want to.

In the quest to change your life, it is important first to understand the challenges you are facing. As mentioned earlier, the first step to achieving a goal is achieving the goal. So, to change your life, you need to identify the areas that need change. In this case, we are going to focus on several problems, including anxiety, depression, panic disorders, and anger.

Everyone, regardless of age, can experience mental disorders, teenagers as young as twelve years have been found to suffer from depression.

Depression

Have you ever felt blue? Or has life ever thrown you a challenge so big that you wanted to quit? There must be at least one event in your life where you felt unsure, thus sunk into confusion. Do not be discouraged because you are not alone. All of us have faced challenges that made us question our abilities. However, we are normally able to sort these issues out and move on. Feelings of sadness only last for a short while then we get back to normal life. However, there are people who cannot get past these feelings of blueness and sadness and can suffer depression.

Clinical depression involves having feelings of extreme sadness that seems endless. In fact, these feelings are so intense that they interfere with normal life activities. Being sad, insecure, and unsure for a long time can make one doubt him/herself, have low self-esteem, reduced confidence, and poor motivation. Depression affects the victim and his/her loved ones. Depression is a serious challenge, and one might miss the signs. Sometimes the signs of depressions are so subtle that one will only discover them only if he/she is on the lookout. Many a time, we ignore depression and go untreated for long periods, thus cannot progress in life as we want. Luckily, depression is treatable, and cognitive behavioral therapy is one of the most effective treatments.

There are numerous causes of depression, and they vary for every person. An event that could cause depression to one person might be seen as irrelevant by the other. For instance, while a grown-up may not be too concerned about fitting in, a teenager may suffer from depression if he/she is neglected by friends. Majorly, the causes of depression can be classified into three; biological, behavioral, and environmental. Understanding the things that might trigger depression can help you to build a better relationship with yourself. Furthermore, you will be able to identify areas of weakness and how to change them.

Below are some of the main and common causes of depression and their recommended solutions;

1. Lack of rewarding experiences
Human beings are designed to pursue success, and we derive a lot of self-pride through achievement. If one loses, there are chances of feeling worthless and gradually heading into depression. Lac of rewarding experiences can take several forms. For instance, the loss of a loved one or a position at work. Such experiences are very unrewarding, and we look for

ways to fill the arising void. If we do not find a replacement, we might head into depression.

Participating in things we like to do gives us a sense of happiness and reward. When we are unable to participate in activities that give us pleasure, it creates a feeling of loss. Here is the sad thing; feeling of sadness makes us unable to participate in pleasurable activities. And being unable to enjoy what we like makes us sadder. Consequently, we get into a cycle of sadness and depression.

Again, appraising oneself is very important. Your relationship with yourself is very crucial for a healthy life, and if it is lacking, you are at risk of depression. If you fail to reward yourself for a job done well, that might trigger depression.

The solution

To deal with this cause of depression, you need to identify those activities that bring you happiness and partake in them. Even when you feel down because of loss, for instance of a loved one, avoid getting into that shell of self-pity. Push yourself to go out. Depression tends to make a person stay away from others. When suffering from depression, you may feel like sleeping all day, and eating junk food is the only viable option offering the needed soothing feeling. However, that is not a solution to depression. The more you hide, the more this disorder thrives.

Ensure that you have a support circle that will reach out for you if you act weird. If you are suffering from depression today, can your best friend know? Things you do under normal circumstances can be very hard when depression strict. Motivating yourself to stay lively during moments of sadness is hard, but you must do it.

2. Failing to use appropriate problem-solving skills.

In most cases, when we face tough challenges, the feeling of helplessness overwhelms us. The mind is capable of making a mole whole to seem like a mountain, and the more you look at a situation with fear or self-doubt, the harder it seems. Thinking about these problems can lead to depression. If you do not have the right mentality and problem-solving skills, life will present you with a situation that might lead to depression.

To deal with problems effectively and avoid going into depression, you need to take an active role. No matter how hard a situation appears to be, do not allow feelings of helplessness to overwhelm you. Consciously choose to be positive and find solutions to these challenges. Chang your orientation towards these situations. Instead of accepting to be the victim, be the problem solver. If things do not work out as you hoped for, do not just sit there and be helpless. Assess the ways you can solve problems and know that no challenge is permanent. If someone is not treating you right, do not sit there and sulk about it, rather, face them.

3. Major changes

There is a saying that states, "The only thing that is constant in life is the change." We are always changing, and so is the world around us. If one does not acknowledge that change will come, he/she might get depressed when it finally comes. There are some major changes in life that can devastate a person, for instance, the loss of a loved one.

Such changes need skills in order to handle them. The best way to avoid going into depression in the event of major changes is to acknowledge that changes will occur and in unexpected ways. Have more acceptances in your life. Let go of too many expectations and just flow with it.

4. Feeling helpless

Feelings of helplessness are bound to arise in our lives every now and then, especially when we are facing major challenges. When these feelings are extremely intense, they might lead us to depression. The main challenge with feeling helpless is that it makes everything to seem impossible. In fact, one might give up on life because there seems to be no light at the end of the tunnel.

To solve this trigger, you need to start thinking of situations differently. If a situation seems to be too tough for you, think of it as a lesson instead of a challenge. Share your problems with your close friends and allow them to give possible solutions. You might release that whatever seemed so hard is actually very easy. Again, do not use generalities to think. Think of each problem in its own aspect. Combining problems can make things to appear harder than they really are. Again, do not limit your options. Consider all the possible solutions, even those that sound absurd.

5. Passivity

Do you ask for what you want or would rather be quiet about it instead of disrespecting" people? Some of us feel like it is wrong to ask for what we want. In fact, there are people who would rather faint out of thirst instead of asking for water. If you do not ask for what you want, you will never get it. And filing to get what you want will only lead you to depression.

Do not stay passive in your life. The things you are afraid of are imaginary. They are just invalids thoughts raised in a platform of emotions. The best solution for passivity is self-analysis. Assess your fears and check if they are valid.

Cognitive-behavioral therapy can help one to deal with depression through identification and restructuring of thoughts. One learns how to interpret things objectively, realistically, and positively. CBT also helps one to identify other maladaptive behaviors that make depression worse.

When treating depression, there are other exercises found in cognitive behavioral therapy that one should consider including treatment of insomnia, assertive communication training, social skills training, treatment of other mental disorders that normally accompany depression such as anxiety and anger, identification of goals, et cetera.

Notably, cognitive-behavioral therapy refers to more than one technique that relies on the disorder being treated. The treatment approach will differ for each mental disorder. For the same mental health condition, the treatment will vary according to the case at hand. It is critical that the therapist commands a knowledge of the particular cognitive-behavioral therapy techniques effective against social anxiety disorder.

Objectives for cognitive behavioral therapy anxiety

The objectives of this therapy are to have the patient working on several areas that are related to building the social confidence and social skills of an individual.

- ❖ How to become more assertive. Becoming assertive is important as it helps define the limits that one can take.
- ❖ Misperceptions that one may have concerning their abilities and self-worth
- ❖ Embarrassment, guilt, or anger over past situations
- ❖ Being more realistic and tackling perfectionism
- ❖ Handling procrastination linked to social anxiety

Benefits of Cognitive behavioral therapy

Cognitive behavioral therapy has been very effective in treating some mental health problems. In some cases, it has been as effective as medications. However, there are some cases where it did not work thus not suitable for everyone.

Some of the cases where Cognitive behavioral therapy can be used successfully include:

- ❖ Where medication alone has not proven helpful
- ❖ Where other forms of therapy have not been effective
- ❖ Where the people involved have limited time

Cognitive behavioral therapy is also preferred because it can be offered in different formats depending on the flexibility of the patient and therapist. There are options such as group therapies, self-help books, applications, and individual therapies. Another advantage of cognitive therapy is that the learned techniques and strategies can be used in daily life even after the treatment sessions are over.

Before using this cognitive behavioral therapy, a person should also know that he/she:

- ❖ Needs to commit him/herself to the process wholesomely to get the maximum benefits. Everything might be laid out clearly, but if the patient fails to cooperate, it might not be helpful.
- ❖ Has to attend a number of sessions and carry out extra work given between sessions. This might take a lot of time.
- ❖ Might experience a season of emotional discomfort and anxiousness in the initial stages because one is required to confront his/her anxieties and emotions.

Due to the structured nature of the therapy sessions, cognitive behavioral therapy may not be best suited for people with learning difficulties and highly complex mental health needs.

Cognitive behavioral therapy mostly relies on a person's ability and capacity to change him/herself; that is, feelings, thoughts, and behaviors. It fails to address more problems in the life of a person, such as family issues and system, which often have a great impact on the health and well-being of a person.

Some therapists also state that Cognitive behavioral therapy is slightly challenged because it only addresses current problems, therefore, leaving out other underlying problems such as troubled childhood.

Unlike other traditional psychotherapy techniques such as that Freudian psychoanalysis which is based on probing the childhood of an individual in order to get the cause of conflicts within the person, Cognitive behavioral therapy focuses on solutions. It encourages the patient to challenge the distorted cognitions and consequently change any destructive patterns of behavior.

Cognitive behavioral therapy is rooted in the idea that perceptions and thoughts are the main influencers of behavior. Feelings such as distress may distort the perception of reality. Hence, CBT identifies harmful thoughts, assesses their validity and accuracy, and if they are inaccurate, the therapy employs strategies to overcome them.

Over the years, Cognitive behavioral therapy has been used for people of all ages, adults, adolescents and even children. It has also been effective when used on face to face basis, online sessions, and even self-treatment. However, having sessions with a therapist to guide the patient has so far proven to be the best way to go. Generally, CBT is a short term therapy that normally ranges from five to twenty sessions. To determine the number of sessions one will require, there are different factors to consider such as

- the severity of the symptoms,
- type of disorder,
- the surrounding situations,
- The rate at which the patient makes progress.
- How long the person has been dealing with the situation,
- The amount of stress a person is experiencing,
- The amount of support the patient gets from family members and other people.

Cognitive behavioral therapy may not cure a condition entirely, but there is the assurance that one will learn how to cope with any unpleasant situations in a better and healthier way. A person will feel better about self and life.

Getting the most

Cognitive behavioral therapy is not effective for everyone, but one can take certain steps to get the most out of the therapy sessions and make successful progress.

Firstly, be honest. When dealing with something stressful and deep, most people tend to lie to other people and even themselves. When using CBT, you have to be honest and open with yourself and with the people helping you.

As mentioned earlier, cognitive behavioral therapy is focused on thoughts, believes, and attitudes. These aspects affect and influence each other. For instance, how does thinking influence negativity in a person's life? Negative thinking patterns can begin as early as childhood. For instance, a person who felt neglected from a tender age, or one who was not praised by parents and teachers from school might develop an inferiority state which leads to negativity. Negative thoughts might develop from mentalities such as 'I'm not good enough'.

As time goes by and one becomes an adult, these negative thoughts become automatic. Consequently, the behavior is influenced by this negativity. The way one thinks affects the behavior in school, at home and general life. Using Cognitive behavioral therapy, one combines cognitive therapy which examines the things one thinks about and behavioral therapy examining the things one does. From that analysis, one is able to take corrective measures.

As indicated, cognitive-behavioral therapy entails a number of methods, most of which focus on problematic thinking. In interpersonal relationships and groups, cognitive methods lessen anxiety and make the person feel that they have regained control over their anxiety in social situations. The primary objective of cognitive therapy is to change the underlying core beliefs that influence how one interprets their surroundings and context. Sufferers of social anxiety are routinely forced to confront their fears, whether real or imaginary, and asking them to toughen up is counterproductive. Such people should be slowly introduced to mild forms of their worst fears until they become completely desensitized to the phobias. Moving exposure train fast will backfire as the mind does not adjust instantly to trained phobias.

There is also interceptive exposure, which is a therapy that helps neutralize as opposed to controlling internal sensations as the patient is systematically exposed to internal sensations in a manner similar to cognitive-behavioral therapy for those with panic disorder.

Limitations

There are a significant number of patients with cognitive-behavioral therapy that do not positively respond to cognitive-behavioral therapy akin to pharmacological treatments. Additionally, patients that respond to cognitive-behavioral therapy occasionally show residual symptoms. Even though cognitive-behavioral therapy is not a limitation on its account alone, but the failure of broader dissemination inhibits the success and usefulness of the technique. Most individuals with social anxiety disorder complain of receiving unstudied psychotherapies that include supportive therapy compared to cognitive-behavioral therapy. There is a need for improvement.

Interpersonal therapy

Notably, interpersonal therapy takes into consideration the social factors that contribute to disorders. The therapy takes into view personal relationships and their impact on social phobia. The therapist determines the social areas that need improvement. The therapy also focuses on helping one improve the relationship with other people. Having social anxiety implies having difficulties and extreme fears when in social circles and interpersonal therapy targets ways of relating in social settings.

Four areas are usually eligible for treatment in the interpersonal therapy model. These areas include role transitions, interpersonal disputes, interpersonal deficits, and grief. The therapist will assist the patient to figure out how individual misconceptions are playing an impact on his or her relationships. Sometimes the patient might not have an objective examination of the situation, and the therapist helps the individual navigate this shortcoming. The patient and the therapist will take role-playing in interpersonal situations to enable them to view the contexts differently. An example is where when you attempt to make a conversation with a stranger. In this manner, role-playing can help act as an unstructured mild form of exposure.

Additionally, the therapist will assist the patient to express and manage their emotions to make changes in their life. Encouragement is important as most patients may show low self-esteem or lack clarification. The current research on interpersonal therapy for treating social phobia indicates that its efficacy is at 78% with some patients reporting positive changes such as finding a new job, dating or returning to school. In some studies, interpersonal therapy was shown to post better outcomes for social anxiety disorder compared to psychodynamic psychotherapy but lesser outcomes when compared to cognitive-behavioral treatment.

Acceptance and commitment therapy treatment

This can be used to treat social anxiety disorder and was based on the relational frame theory. The acceptance and commitment therapy shares many of the values of the Buddhist philosophy. The overall goal of acceptance and commitment therapy is to encourage the processing of negative thoughts instead of the elimination or reduction of them. Since not everyone responds to cognitive-behavioral therapy, acceptance and commitment therapy could be a critical alternative therapy to treating social anxiety disorder. The acceptance and commitment therapy argues that one's normal routine thoughts can become damaging. The acceptance and commitment treatment assumes that language is the cause of human suffering as it is the basis for negative thoughts and emotions such as obsession, prejudice, self-criticism, and fear.

Correspondingly, the goal of acceptance and commitment therapy is not to eliminate social anxiety symptoms as trying to directly control or lessen the symptoms will actually make them worse. Through this acceptance and commitment therapy, one will be encouraged to enjoy a meaningful life, accept that there will always be pain and suffering and that one should detach from it and take action based on the values. In overall, the acceptance and commitment therapy will make the social and anxiety symptoms become less.

Relatedly, acceptance, and commitment therapy builds on six principles. Firstly, there is cognitive diffusion which entails detaching oneself from unpleasant private experiences like feelings, thoughts, memories, images, sensations and urges. A person will always have experiences, but the intent of acceptance and commitment therapy is to lessen the influence that the experiences have on the person. The inherent reaction is to struggle against unpleasant experiences, but doing so will only worsen them. The therapist may point out how struggling against negative feelings is akin to trying to climb out of quicksand. The other principles include acceptance, contact with the present moment, observing self, values, and committed action.

Cognitive behavioral therapy has developed over the years and become helpful to very many people. Mental disorders such as post-traumatic stress disorder, depression, obsessive-compulsive disorders, and generalized anxiety disorder create a continuous negative feedback loop making a person unhealthy. In most cases, these disorders require direct intervention to stop the vicious cycle. Without the appropriate intervention, the bothersome fears and beliefs will continue to preoccupy the mind of the affected person and threaten to rule his/her life. Since human beings are wired to focus on fears more than positivity, they are easily distracted when negative things come to fruition. These occurrences reinforce negative thoughts.

Thankfully, cognitive behavioral therapy has provided patients and psychologists with ways to interrupt this cycle and achieve positive and healthy thinking patterns. It is important to understand the stages of Cognitive behavioral therapy.

Basically, there are four main stages in CBT treatment namely assessment stage, cognitive stage, behavioral stage, and learning stage. These stages apply depending on whether you are using the help of a therapist or you are using the therapy on your own. In this book, we will look at two stages; the one where a person identifies negative thought patterns and the one where he/she changes them

Identifying negative thoughts

The bottom line of cognitive behavioral therapy is identifying negative thought patterns and changing them to healthy options. In simpler terms, this therapy helps you change your internal dialogue. Negative thinking is defined as thinking that results in negative consequences. Such thinking normally ignores important facts and focuses on a few selective and negative facts or false beliefs. Normally, negative thinking is absolute, rigid and unsupported by facts.

Whenever your thinking is rigid and irrational, one tends to take an all or nothing approach in life. Things become black and white and the person resists change, for instance, a person might focus on the false belief that he/she is stupid, therefore, if anyone tries to convince him/her otherwise, she will not believe. Sometimes, people have a hard time recognizing negative thinking. All they notice is that their life is not working properly and it feels like something in life is stuck. Cognitive behavioral therapy should help you identify your thought patterns and develop healthy ones. There are various types of negative thinking and some overlap each other. The main ones include;

First, there is the all- or – nothing thinking whereby the person thinks that he/she has to do things perfectly and anything less than that is a failure.

Secondly, there is focusing on the negative things in life. A person may feel that nothing goes his/her way, concentrating on things that did not work to make life hard for the people with negative mentalities.

Thirdly, there is negative elf labeling whereby a person brands him/herself with negative things. One might think that if people knew his/her weaknesses, they would not talk to him/her.

Finally, there are those people who catastrophize everything. They always think of the worst case scenario.

Other negative mentalities include:

Excessive need for approval, - There are people who believe that they can only be happy if someone else loves them. Such thoughts can limit the ability of a person to live happily

Mindreading- there are people who believe that they can tell how other people perceive them because of the way they behave.

The 'should' statement- Some people believe that things should be done in a particular way and anything less is a failure. When other people do things differently, the person affected by such negative thoughts thinks that they are unfair.

Disqualifying the present – some people feel that they cannot relax at the moment, therefore, they need to rush to and do another thing here and there. It is more like life cannot go on without their intervention.

Other people dwell on the past too much. In fact, they concentrate on the negative things that happened years back. They feel that life would be better if a certain thing had not happened the way they did.

Pessimism is also a common form of negative thoughts. Some people feel that they will never be happy, and things will never get better. Such thoughts pull people down.

Basically, no one is born with negative thinking. Many people learn it as they grow up. The people one socializes with, the places he/she visits, and things experienced can determine how one sees life. If you are surrounded by negativity, then it seems normal. You will hardly question if it is right and healthy or not. You will not even question where you learned it from. It feels like the norm – how you have always done it.

Negative thinking becomes automatic thinking through repeated practice. As you apply negative thinking, it becomes a natural way of doing things. Gradually, it feels like part of you and no better way of doing things. You then automatically assume that you are a failure.

Automatic thoughts are helpful in our day to day lives because there are minor decisions we do not need to ponder much. It would be tiresome to have to think keenly for every choice we make. Automatic thoughts help you to navigate through life efficiently. However, automatic thoughts are unhelpful if your assumptions are based on false beliefs. If your thoughts are mostly negative, then you will keep coming up with the wrong decisions and conclusions without understanding why.

Luckily, what you have learned can be unlearnt. You can learn a different way of thinking. That is the aim of cognitive behavioral therapy – to help a person recognize and let go of the negative mentalities and apply positive ones. Learning better ways of thinking will help you lead a better life.

The consequences of negative thinking can be very drastic; therefore the need to unlearn it and adopt rationality. You see, the consequences of negative thinking tend to accumulate. For instance, one negative thought piles on the others. In time, these thoughts take a toll on the way you view life, future and yourself. If you have the all or nothing mentality, you will have anxiety disorders. Your worries that making mistakes will expose you to judgment or criticism will make you fail more. As such, you will have more anxiety and lack time to relax and let your guard down.

If you think that you are damaged, unfixable and unlikable, chances are, you will get depressed. You will be trapped by your own unrealistic view of self. One major cause of depressions is the feeling of being trapped.

Negative thinking will lead to depression or anxiety, which will further lead to addiction. Anxiety, depression and other mental disorders feel so uncomfortable that you might seek comfort from in drugs alcohol and other negative practices.

Negative thinking will not only block your happiness but also obstruct self-change. When you think of life as an all or nothing assignment, then even a small change might feel like a burden or irrelevance. You cannot see the way to making small changes, and the big ones seem too huge for you. You lack the means and strength.

To change the mentality, you will need to have a way of recording and analyzing your thoughts. One way of keeping track of your thoughts is through journalizing. As mentioned earlier, journalizing helps a person understand his/her thoughts, feelings and emotions. When you put things down, you understand the things that trigger your fears, depression, anxiety, phobias, et cetera.

The other way of keeping track of your thoughts is through Cognitive behavioral therapy worksheets. They are also referred to as thought records because they help one to think about his/her thinking patterns. Basically, the record of the thoughts is a basic tool of cognitive therapy. It involves a series of questions leading you step by step through the process of assessing, and identifying your negative thoughts and changing them.

The cognitive behavioral sheet helps you to reflect on our thinking after writing down the facts of your reactions. You are able to acknowledge your anger, fear, depression, phobia, et cetera, thus it is easier to identify the thinking challenge. A thought record also helps you recognize the false nature of core beliefs. You realize that most of your negative thoughts are untested and unwarranted. For instance, you might believe that you are a failure just because someone told you that when you were growing up. You actually might be the best in what you do but still, feel unworthy because of the belief. That is a classic example of false beliefs. You have not stopped to challenge the line of thought which you learned at a young age. Thought records / cognitive behavioral therapy worksheets help you to find healthier ways of gathering the facts. You could not see the rational thoughts because they differed from what you learned as a child. You can change your thinking. And the realization that change is possible is the first step towards real change. Once you change your thinking, you change your life.

Some of the content you can find in a thought record template includes:

i. The situation – This is a record of circumstances that lead to unpleasant feelings. It will help you recall things in a better way when you review your notes later.

ii. The initial thought – What was your first thought when the situation arose? It probably is an automatic thought which you have had before and

iii. The consequences. – If you want to change your thoughts, what are the possible consequences? If you fail to change, what will be the consequences? Consider all consequences, physical, mental, emotional, professional, and relational.

Basically, the first three steps help you identify what you need to change. They also give you the motivation to change.

iv. Challenge your initial thoughts – You need to ask yourself how helpful your thoughts have been. Do you have the facts to support or challenge your thoughts? Which strengths are you overlooking that might help you overcome the negative thoughts? What would you tell a person in the same situation as you are?

v. Negative thinking – Write down the negative thoughts behind your initial thought. It could be the all or nothing mentality, catastrophizing, focusing on negativity or self-labeling. You will notice that the same type of negative thought keeps coming up.

vi. Background – Try to remember the first time you had these feelings. What is the root cause? Are they from your childhood, or did you learn them along the way? Do you know anyone else who thinks like this either in the family or outside?

Have they succeeded with this kind of thinking? Steps five and six help one to identify that negative thinking is based on false assumptions rather than facts. You will also be able to learn the background of your thoughts.

vii. Alternative thinking - Since the previous steps have helped you identify the negative thoughts and their background, you now need to state the possible alternative mentalities.

viii. Positive affirmation and belief - Write down a positive form of affirmation that reflects your healthier approach to life. Choose something you can use as a reminder.

Steps seven and eight guides you to come up with healthier ways of thinking and affirming.

ix. Action plan - If this situation arises again, what will you do? How can you prepare for the situation? Which strengths would you bring to the situation? Considering your weaknesses, strengths, and tendencies, what can you do avoid falling back to the same habits?

x. Improvement - Do you feel better after following your goals through? This final step helps you to acknowledge that a change in thinking is a change in life.

The last two steps help you to incorporate new thinking into life. Cognitive behavioral therapy is effective because of the step by step processes which allow a person to undergo.

A practical example of a thought record:

i. The situation - I mentioned something weird or wrong at a social event. The first feeling involved embarrassment, and when I thought of it later, I became anxious.

ii. Initial thought - When thinking about it, I first felt like a failure. Then I worried that people would judge me. I hated this feeling and the fact that I am always making dumb mistakes

iii. Consider the consequences - If I continue thinking like this and consistently beating myself up, I will feel miserable. This negativity will affect my relationships and consequently ,my health. If I keep thinking of myself as a failure, I might lose my self-respect and start to act like a failure.

iv. Challenge your initial thoughts - I feel overwhelmed every time I try to do things perfectly. I do not have to be perfect. Every time I beat myself up, I become boring. People who are kinder to themselves have a more fulfilling life, everybody makes mistakes, and it is not a big deal. I need to stop criticizing myself.

v. Negative thinking - I was focusing on the negative things and self-labeling. I was also mind reading that other people do not like me.

vi. Background - I can hear the voices of my teachers, saying that I will always fail.

vii. Alternative thinking - I do not have to do things perfectly. Nobody is perfect. I have some positive aspects appreciated by other people. I want to alter negative thinking because I feel better when I am kind to myself.

viii. Positive belief and affirmation - Everybody makes mistakes; therefore, be kind to yourself.

ix. Action plan - Before going to a social setting, I will consciously remind myself that too much perfection is boring. If I make a mistake, it is okay, and I should not dwell on it. I will remember to be kind to others as well as myself and remind myself of my previous successes.

x. Improvement - Assess your progress. Writing things down will help you monitor your progress.

Stage two

The second stage involves challenging these negative thoughts that we have already identified in stage one. There are different exercises used to change negative thinking in cognitive behavioral therapy. They have been developed over the years and are used to solve some of the most complicated mental disorders.

Simply put, Cognitive behavioral therapy begins with simplified ways of understanding difficult and challenging situations and how a person reacts to them. The focus is on problematic reactions such as negative thinking which leads to deeper problems such as depression, anxiety, and phobias. The concepts of this therapy are based on three components involved in psychological problems: emotions, thoughts, and behaviors. When a person breaks down the feelings into these components, he/she understands where and how to intervene. If a particular thought seems negative and is causing a chain of reactions in behavior and emotions, the first and best step is to examine and reexamine. To change the behavioral pattern, you need to learn new ones.

Researchers have found that the three components, emotions, thoughts and behaviors are normally intertwined throughout the difficult problems and feelings. As such, cognitive behavioral therapy is designed to deal with all the components simultaneously. For example, when a person has uncontrollable worry, the cognitive behavioral therapy helps him/her to identify some more rational thoughts, which in turn result in a reduction of anxiety. Further, the reduced anxiety makes it easier for the person to engage in skillful behavior which actively addresses the problematic situation that triggered the anxiety in the first place. Below is a list of exercises used in cognitive behavioral therapy to help resolve negative thoughts.

a. Cognitive restructuring

This is an exercise designed to help a person examine unhelpful thinking patens and come up with new ways of reacting when problematic situations arise. Normally, cognitive restructuring involves keeping a record of thoughts, which allows a person to track patterns and changes in thoughts. From this record, a person can devise adaptive alternative responses for every situation.

    b.   Activity scheduling this involves planning for a person to engage in activities he/she would not engage in ordinarily, due to depression, stress, fear, anxiety et cetera.

This form of intervention involves identifying a low frequency yet rewarding behavior and finding time to do it frequently throughout the week. The scheduling has to be deliberate, and the person has to be willing to do it in order to reap the benefits. Activity scheduling is often used to treat depression. Normally, a depressed person will stop engaging in rewarding activities as he/she spends more time brooding on negative thoughts. Activity schedules will ensure that a person gradually becomes active again.

Studies have found that reactivating rewarding behavior is a very viable way of treating some mental disorders such as anxiety, phobia and more so depression. In fact, it has been found to be as effective as antidepressant medication in some cases. Activity scheduling is effective in reducing depressive symptoms, and psychiatrists have found it even more efficient than medication when keeping the depression symptoms from recurring after treatment.

The idea behind activity scheduling and behavioral activation is that when a person is suffering from depression, (depressive cycle) he/she slowly withdraws from the rewarding activities. You will realize that a depressed person will spend too much time watching TV or just staying in bed when other people are working. They also tend to avoid people and activities that would benefit them. Behavioral activation involves planning and reintroducing these rewarding activities into the life of the person. These activities can either be mastery oriented such as painting or learning a musical instrument, or pleasurable such as going out with a friend, taking a walk, going shopping, et cetera. One may also choose to volunteer at a charity. Gradually, after a period of engaging in these reinforced activities, the moods will improve, and the self-defeating thoughts will reduce. The upward mood cycle will build momentum.

The basic way of activating behavior is through activity scheduling and monitoring. You will need to keep a detailed record of activities and behavior, and also the feelings and emotions of pleasure and mastery linked to each behavior. This will help you to analyze what might be missing from your schedule. After tracking your activities and behaviors for some days or weeks, you will spend the next weeks increasing the rewarding behaviors into your life. Identify new rewarding behaviors and incorporate them into your schedule.

This way, the patient will come out of the depressive cycle by replacing negative thoughts with positive and rewarding patterns. Contentment cycles help to treat depression. Although behavioral activation and scheduling sounds like an easy thing, remember that even a simple and pleasurable activity can be burdensome to a depressed person. One might lack the motivation. It is therefore important to have a person who knows about behavioral activation and its barriers helping you. One needs to know the techniques for aiding change, avoiding pitfalls, and reaching a goal. Some people feel the benefits of Behavioral activation after the first sessions, while others take a longer time. Regardless of your timing, do not quit.

    c. Graded exposure

In cognitive behavioral therapy, exposure refers to an exercise designed to reduce fear and anxiety through contact with what one is afraid of. Researchers have found this exercise to be among the most effective treatment formulae for psychological problems. The underlying idea is that the more we avoid what we fear, we increase the levels of anxiety. A systematic approach towards what you fear will help you deal with anxiety and other psychological problems.

For example, someone who suffers from dog phobia can face dogs gradually. For people with social anxiety, the challenge is meeting people and being in the presence of new people. The way to solve social anxiety is through gradually meeting and talking to people.

    d. Successive approximation

This is a cognitive behavioral therapy exercise used to help people deal with difficult or overwhelming goals. The basic idea behind successive approximation is breaking down any large tasks into smaller manageable steps. Also, a person can perform a task that is almost similar to the goal but less challenging. Consequently, he/she will learn the mastery needed for the bigger goal.

e. Mindfulness meditation

This is an exercise that helps people to disengage from harmful obsessing or ruminating and learn to connect with the present moment. Originally, mindfulness originates from Buddhist meditation. It is rooted in significant research on treatments of psychological problems.

Basically, mindfulness techniques seek to develop an awareness of feelings and thoughts without judgment or attachment. When a person is caught up in intense emotions, it is often because of a catastrophic imagination and interpretation about the things going on. The more we overthink about a situation, the worse it feels thus, our emotions become overwhelming. Mindfulness cuts this process short and helps us disentangle ourselves from the distorted thoughts and engage in the current moment. Being in the moment helps one address the current challenges in a more skillful way, with less psychological suffering and emotional reactivity.

One of the exercises that a person can pratice to become more mindful is meditation. From meditation to visualization, different forms of meditations have been developed over the years with the intention of enhancing compassion, serenity, and wisdom. However, in recent years, modern science has recognized that meditation has positive impacts on the brain. These benefits include increased emotion regulation, better immune system functionality, and improved attention. As a result, even people who are not connected to spiritual worlds have begun to reap the benefits from meditation.

Mindfulness is basically a form of meditation, and its purpose is to bring the whole mind into the present moment in a wholesome manner. Mindfulness ensures that pone is not distracted by unrelated thoughts and judgments. In most cases, we are caught up in thought unrelated to our current situation and we hardly realize so. This preoccupation has many negative effects, the main one being that we are unable to make the most of our current moment. We are unable to enjoy the moment fully. According to researches, our moods can take a significant dip when we are preoccupied. On the other hand, when our mind is concentrating on the present, we are able to appreciate the moment and our moods improve significantly.

There are various ways of practicing mindfulness. Listed below are instructions on how you can become mindful through the simple practice of breathing.

- ❖ Find a quiet place. Ensure that the place is free of distractions because the mind tends to form its own. A place with significant destruction will make sustaining attention more difficult.
- ❖ Sit down and close your eyes. There is no particular way of sitting down. Just ensure that you are comfortable. The sitting position should not be distracting you.

❖ Bring your thoughts to the breathing sensation you are getting as air enters and exits the nose. The best part of this exercise is that it is simple and has no complex steps for you to visualize. However, you will realize that it is hard because your mind keeps wandering to other things such as planning, physical sensation, rehashing past events and daydreaming.

The bottom line is to focus on the breathing process and nothing else. Distraction should be expected and as you get better at mindfulness, you will notice when your mind wanders off. All that is required of you is to bring your mind back to this moment. Gently let go of the distractions and breathe. Again and again. If you have to bring your mind back 100 times in one minute, do it and do not give up. You will feel discouraged if your mind keeps drifting to other things but understand that at least you have learned how to notice distractions. Formerly, you were distracted but did not notice.

Keep watching your breath for about five minutes and note when distraction occurs. Bring your mind to the present every time you have to and do not give up. Afterward, you will notice a sense of calmness taking over after taking the exercise.

As you become more connected with the mindfulness practice, you can increase the meditation time to 10, 15, 20 minutes. The key to success is consistency. It is better to meditate for five minutes every day than one hour, once a week.

Try this exercise and take note of the changes you will notice. Gradually, you will have the ability to concentrate on what you are doing. If you are eating, your mind will be able to focus on the process of chewing, swallowing, and tasting, Et cetera. If you are driving, mindfulness will enable you to focus on the current ride. Focus on connecting to the present moment.

f. Skills training

This is an exercise used to remedy skills deficit, and it works through direct instructions, modeling, and role-plays. The most common subjects in skills training are assertive training, social skills training and communication training.

g. Problem-solving

This is an exercise in therapy used to help people take an active role in getting solutions for problems. There are aspects of life that might lead a person to take a passive role. For instance, repeated disappointments in life and chronic mood problems make a person feel helpless when a difficult situation arises. When you teach a person effective problem-solving skills, It becomes easier for him/her to gain control and get the best out of a difficult situation.

h. Relaxation breathing training

This exercise is designed to help a person take control of the physiological symptoms of anxiety such as rapid heart rate, shortness of breath, dizziness, et cetera. By reducing the arousal of the body, a person is able to think more clearly, thus decreasing the symptoms of anxiety while increasing feelings of comfort. After understanding the different types of negative thoughts, there are questions you can ask yourself to challenge the negative self-talk and thoughts.

- ❖ First, ask you-in my current thoughts, am I falling into any negative thoughts category, for instance personalizing or catastrophizing?
- ❖ Do any facts support my current thoughts, or am I just assuming?
- ❖ Which facts can prove that my thoughts are not true?
- ❖ Have I confused a fact with a thought?
- ❖ What can a friend say about my thoughts if he/she knew about them?
- ❖ What could I tell a friend if he/she was in the same situation?
- ❖ Is it really important in my life?
- ❖ What is the probability that my fears will come true?
- ❖ Have I been in the same situation before? What were the results? If not, do I know someone who has been there before?
- ❖ If my fears come to pass, what is my plan for dealing with it?
- ❖ Is my judgment really rational?
- ❖ Between possibility and certainty, which option is more applicable in my case?

Chapter 2: Goal Setting

Setting a goal might sound like an easy task, and truth be told, it is the easiest step in any process. However, it is the most crucial step and will determine if you succeed or fail. Although we are focusing on setting goals about personal development, dealing with depression, anger, anxiety, panic attacks, among other disorders, the below-listed steps can be used to set other life goals.

The first step in goal setting is to identify the goal. Would you like to handle your anger more effectively? Or do you want to get over those feelings of anxiety? Would you like to help a friend get past depression? Or are you trying to understand the causes of panic attacks? Whatever your goal is, you must identify it. That will be the director of your actions.

The second step is identifying a starting point. They say that the hardest part of anything is starting. To achieve your goals, you need to identify a starting point. What is your current situation, and how can you use it to achieve your goal? Or instance, if you want to manage your anger, how are you currently managing? Are there things you need to understand in your background? Which steps can you take to make your situation better? When assessing a starting point, it is important, to be honest with yourself.

Thirdly, identify your steps.

What steps can you take towards your goals? It is hard to achieve a goal in one step, especially when it comes to changing oneself. Our beliefs and personalities are formed over the years, and some of them are planted so deeply within us. You cannot change a core belief overnight. So, what are the steps you need to take in order to reach your goals? Break those steps into small and achievable tasks. A long term goal can seem like a far off hard challenge, but if you break it down into short term, achievable goals, with sensible timeframes, these goals become more realistic. Every time you achieve one of the shorter-term goals, it acts as a stepping stone to the next and a crucial motivating factor.

Be attentive with your first steps because they can either build or destroy your esteem. It is important to put your steps in order according to what you want to achieve first. And know that every victory will motivate you.

While setting your steps, consider the obstacles that might arise, and brace yourself for them. Work your way around every hindrance. Though you might not be prepared for every obstacle that will occur along the way, at least have some backup information to help.

In order to achieve more in life, your goals must be smart, that is, specific, measurable, achievable, relevant, and timely.

By specific we mean, your goals should have a clear direction such that you can tell if you are on the right track or not. Being specific ensures that you are surer about what you want. For instance, if you want to lose weight, it will be better if you clearly know what you must do. You could be clearer about weight loss by knowing exactly how you will do it, for instance, through dieting and going to the gym. It is even better if you know the exact number of times you will be going to the gym and the foods you will be consuming. So, instead of saying "my aim is to lose weight" you can say, i need to lose weight, by going to the gym, thrice a week for two hours and watching my diet. I will only consume..." This way, you know exactly what is required.

Measurable goals mean having steps that you can assess clearly. For instance, in the weight loss example, one must know the exact number of times he/she will be going to the gym. If it is three times, you will know when you have achieved your goals or not at the end of the week. However, if one just says he/she wants to go to the gym and leaves that goal at that point, it will be hard to measure achievements.

Achievable goals mean that you can actually attain them. It is pointless to set a goal such as learning how to fly a plane in two days because that is hardly achievable- well unless we are talking of toy ones. However, you can say that you will learn to drive in three months. It is good to have aspirations but setting unachievable goals might do you more harm than good. They might kill your self-esteem.

Relevant goals mean that whatever you are aiming for is in line with your long term goals and life at large. Which problems are you addressing? Do your current goals help you to find a solution to the problems you are facing? If you want to build a better social life, are you learning about communication skills?

Timely goals mean doing the right thing at the right time. A goal can be perfect, but trying to achieve it in the wrong timeframe can lead to more harm than good. For instance, if you want to learn how to ride a bike, but you have a back injury, this might not be the best time.

After defining your personal core values that you want to be central in your life, you now need to use these values to guide a list of actions you need to take. Even though it is crucial to gain knowledge of your personal core values, it will be a waste of time if you don't act on these values to live by. You should start to make the conscious choice as well as the commitment to practice every value you hold dear through your actions.

Committed action could mean engaging in general patterns of effective actions, which are influenced by your personal core values. Flexibility and adaptability are crucial for committed action to be effective. This will allow you to easily adapt to any change in your life without compromising your values.

But regardless of how many lapses you commit, you should never give up. You need to review your actions and have them aligned with your values.

By gaining a deeper understanding of your values, you can start setting goals for your life that are based on these values. For instance, if you value hard work, a solid goal can help you become more productive and efficient in the workplace. Your goals in life will definitely change as the needs arise, while values should be consistent and should be used as your motivational boost in guiding how you behave.

In the ACT context, committed action has four steps:

1. Select a specific aspect of your life that you really want to change
2. Select the personal core values you like to pursue in this area in your life
3. Establish goals that are based on your values
4. Mindfully take the necessary actions

The bigger objective of transforming values into committed action is to live a life that is filled with purpose, which is guided by the values that are important to you. If you think that your life is going nowhere or out of balance, it is possible that these feelings are caused by not acting based on your values or being out of touch with your core values. When you become mindful of your actions, you can start to take the needed steps to transform these values into committed action.

The ACT Process for Setting up Goals

ACT encourages setting up of goals that are based on values. It specifies three major steps:

Step 1 - Choose an area in your life that you want to work on.

This may include community, romance, education, career, personal growth, environment, family, parenting, health, finances, and many more.

Step 2 - Establish goals that are SMART - Specific, Meaningful, Adaptive, Realistic, and Time-Bound.

Specific - Try to be specific as possible on what actions you want to take. Be sure that you are aware of the involved steps in taking the necessary action. A specific goal is easier to achieve compared to a general goal. For example, just setting up the goal of spending more time with your child may not allow you to know if you have already achieved it. A more specific goal is to spend at least one-hour playtime every day. Being specific with your goal will allow you to assess whether you have already accomplished the goal or not and monitor your progress.

Meaningful - Assess if your goal is genuinely based on your values in comparison with a strict rule or a sense of what you must do. If you think that your goals don't have a deeper sense of purpose or meaning, try to assess if the goal is really influenced by the values you hold dear. Take note that your core values should be based on things that provide meaning to your life.

Adaptive - Make sure that your goal will help you follow a direction that you think will greatly improve your life. Assess if your goal will move you closer or is steering you away from the real purpose of your life.

Realistic - There's a big chance that you will only feel disappointment, frustration, or failure if you have set goals that are not really attainable. You should try to find a balance between setting goals that are quite easy versus goals that are impossible to achieve. Be realistic and practical if you can really push yourself to achieve your goals.

Time-Bound - You can specify your goals even more by adding a time and date by which you want to accomplish the goal. If this is not possible, or not realistic, try setting up a time frame and do everything you can to make certain that you work within this bond.

Step 3 - Define the Urgency of Your Goals

The last step is to define the urgency that your goal should be accomplished. Your goals could be:

- Long-term - Create a plan of the necessary actions you need to take so you can be closer to your goals over the span of six months to one year.

- Medium-term - Think about the necessary actions you need to take so you can move towards your goals within two to three months
- Short-term goals - Make a list of the things you need to do so you can achieve your goals within a month
- Immediate goal - What are the goals that you need to achieve within a week or even within the day?

Starting to live in accordance with your personal core values will fan the flames of your committed action.

Our best plan and values will not be meaningful if they are not supported by action. Equipped with the knowledge of the core values you really want to pursue, you can start moving forward towards living a valuable life.

Chapter 3: Identifying the Obstacles

Emotions are an important part of us as human beings. What would we be, and what would our lives be like, if we are without emotions? Admittedly, emotions do become a problem — or the cause of a multitude of problems — especially if they run amok. Still, they are important, and they have roles to play in our lives. For example, our emotions can motivate us, and they can be the driving force behind our success, helping us overcome obstacles after obstacles. Emotions, when harnessed properly, can also become great tools for communication. An impassioned speech is more likely to trigger action than a dry talk.

Furthermore, our emotions, with proper discernment, can tell us something about our situation or our environment, like when there is some danger that we cannot see.

Our subject here, however, is regulating our emotions, so that our feelings, especially the negative ones, do not get out of hand. And there are indeed some factors that do prevent effective control of our emotions, such as biological factors, lack of skills, emotional overload, and erroneous beliefs.

DBT deals with some of these factors. Emotions are a complex process, and we probably don't need to know how exactly they happen.

What is important for us is to be able to identify their different kinds, because that is the first step towards gaining control. Knowledge is power, as they say.

Do you feel angry, disgusted, or envious? Are you fearful, jealous, or happy? Do you feel shame, or do you feel the love? And why do you think you feel this way?

Changing Emotional Responses

Sometimes, we find the resolve to change our emotional response to a situation, simply because we do not want what we are feeling. It can be anger, shame, guilt, or despair.

The following skills can help you do just that: change your emotions.

Fact checking

This simply means that we should ascertain whether our thoughts, feelings, or behaviors agree, or are reasonable responses to the events that cause them. This is because our own interpretations of events can be wrong and this ,in turn, can cause us to make erroneous responses.

Opposite Action

Opposite action means doing just the opposite of what our present emotion is inciting us to do, which is also called the "action urge" of that particular emotion. For example, if you are feeling angry with someone, your tendency is to attack that person. The opposite action of this is to gently try to avoid the confrontation.

Opposite action, however, is not always the best thing to do, but there are two situations where this is advisable. The first one is when, after checking the facts, you found out that your emotion is an unreasonable response to what has caused it. The second one is when acting on your emotion will not result in anything good, and will probably only worsen the situation. It doesn't matter then if your emotion is justified or not.

Problem Solving

When the emotion you want to change is reasonable or is justified, then what you can do is to either avoid the situation or try to change it — so that your emotion can change too.

Problem solving is to try to change the situation that causes your unwanted emotion. It begins by you identifying the problem by considering all the facts.

Next, you set your goal (one that will make you feel alright), and then you brainstorm and ask advice for possible solutions. Finally, you try out each promising solution until the problem is solved.

Reducing Vulnerability to Emotion Mind

The good news is that, with time and with practice, our resilience to emotional disturbances and our resistance to emotion mind can be built up.

The following skills can help you strengthen your heart, so to speak:

Accumulate Positive Emotions

This is like continually depositing money in the bank, so that when a time of great financial need comes, you have savings to withdraw money from. But instead of money and instead of a real bank, you deposit good emotions and happy experiences in your heart and mind. And so, when a time of crisis, tragedy, or any other difficulty comes, you will have this reservoir of positive energy and positive memories to draw strength from. Accumulating positive emotions has both short-term and long-term goals. In a short-term goal, you do now what you can to experience pleasant things. In a long-term goal, you make some changes in your life so that more good things will happen to you in the future. Extending our analogy, you not only deposit money today, but you also make some investments, so that someday your income will exponentially increase.

Build Mastery and Cope Ahead

Building mastery is doing things that will give you a sense of accomplishment and competence. This can be a new hobby that teaches you skills you don't know before — or anything that stretches you and makes you grow. The confidence that you gain from this will become part of your preparedness to deal with difficult situations.

Coping ahead, on the other hand, is planning and training to deal with the emotional battles when they come. This includes analysis of possible problems, consideration of possible solutions, and even rehearsing in your own mind your possible responses.

Chapter 4: Activate Behavior

Experts of CBT encourage the persistent non-judgmental link between environmental and psychological events as they happen. The objective is for us to feel a more straightforward experience so that we increase the flexibility of our behavior and so our actions could be more aligned with the values that are important to us. We can achieve this by permitting our behavior to be influenced by our workability, and also through language to take note and describe events and not to merely judge or predict them.

A study conducted by Harvard University reveals that humans spend 50% of their time daydreaming. This is a surprising fact considering the limited time we have. Humans have the ability to detach from the present and think over the past or the future. This is considered as a gift because we can revisit our past and learn from it to improve ourselves. This will allow us to grow as individuals and as a society as we can collectively look after our wellbeing.

It also allows us to plan for our future. It is a good thing if we can anticipate what could happen in the next few years to come. Our ability to place ourselves in the possible situation will allow us to think about how we can deal with different circumstances when they happen.

However, if our daydreaming can result in emotional disturbance, they could significantly affect our mental health and steal our happiness. It becomes a burden – a hurdle that we need to overcome.

Too much thinking about the past could lead us down the path of regrets or the inability to accept and let things go. It should not be altogether eliminated because it allows us to plan for the future. However, thinking too much of the future can be a bad thing because it could mean that we are not living our lives to the fullest and that we are wasting our time and energy preparing for scenarios that aren't even likely to happen.

Daniel Gilbert, a renowned psychologist from Harvard University, explores the psychological immune system that activates during stressful events allowing us to cope. More often than not, these things are not as bad as

Remember, habits are actually behaviors that we have learned over time. Hence, we can unlearn these habits by becoming aware of them and being persistent in changing our ways.

The more we give in to our habits, the more they become strong and entrenched in our system. But each time we try to do something that is different from our habits, they will be weaker, and the new behavior will eventually become stronger as you practice them. CBT offers a step-by-step approach to breaking bad habits:

Step 1 - Decide to Make the Decision Today

The very first step in breaking your habit is to make the decision to do something about your bad habit. It is crucial to make the decision today - not tomorrow as it will reinforce within you the determination to change. Once you thought about the damages brought by the habit, you are more driven to do something about it.

Moreover, it is also crucial to focus on the benefits you can obtain when you are successful in breaking the habit. Think about the worst case scenario of going on with the habit, and this could drive you to act on it. You may even resolve to quit the habit right at this first step. There are people who have developed the bad habit of checking their email every five minutes to the point that it has become counterproductive. When you become more aware of why you need to change this habit, it becomes easier to change.

Step 2 - Practice Mindfulness

To put a stop to a bad habit, you must first become aware and accept the fact that your habit is detrimental to yourself as a person. You also need to accept the reality that only you could stop it. It is essential that you are aware of the disadvantages of sticking to your bad habit.

For instance, if you are constantly binge-watching Netflix even on a work night, you need to think about the circumstances that drive you to spend countless hours to watching shows that may not be contributing to your well-being. How do you feel when you wake up in the morning after a night of watching a whole season?

It is crucial to keep track of your habits and get to know the circumstances and frequency when you usually engage in these habits. For example, if you bite your nails, do you do it when you are at home or at work? Also, take note of your emotions when you do this habit.

Carefully study your habit at least weekly. By doing this, you can see an emerging trend and you can discover the antecedents of the behavior. Identify the things that could trigger your habit. What are the environmental triggers that drive you to plunge into your bad habit? By being mindful of your bad habits, the frequency declines, which is an important step in making the much-needed change.

You will find a detailed discussion on Mindfulness in the next chapter, as well as some exercises that could help you become more mindful.

Step 3 - Use CBT Strategies to Change the Habit

Take note that the fundamental concept in CBT revolves around our thoughts, our emotions, and our behavior. The way we think will affect the way we feel and act. Hence, CBT is an effective form of treatment for stopping bad habits.

One effective CBT strategy in dealing with bad habits is the basic STOP technique. Once you become aware that you are doing a bad habit, you need to stop it right away by literally saying STOP to yourself. Some people find it helpful to write the word STOP on a piece of paper and display it near their work area or somewhere that is easily seen, so they are reminded to stop their bad habit right away.

It is also ideal to seek support from a family, friend, or a colleague at work who could observe you and tell you when you are in your bad habit again. Just keep track of your habit, and try to reward yourself for breaking the bad habit.

Also, remember that this is not supposed to be easy. Don't be discouraged, even if you feel that you are not successful. It's possible that your habits may even become worse during the early stages. This could be because you are now trying to monitor something that you were used to doing automatically. It is also possible that mindfulness triggers more tension and anxiety, and the frequency is thus increased. Never give up as this phase will not last long.

Step 4 - Find New Alternatives to Your Bad Habit

If your bad habit involves using your hand, you can try keeping your hands occupied through an alternative activity, so that it will stop you from nail biting or hair pulling. Playing with a stress ball could help.

Women also use manicure products or hand cream to resolve their nail-biting habits, while some who habitually rub their eyes wear makeup, so they are discouraged from do the habit. Be sure that you are aware of the specific types of feelings that trigger you to do bad habits.

If you know that it is boredom, worry, anxiety, or tension, then try doing something about this specific emotional trigger.

Of gossiping, then try to become more mindful if you are sharing a story that is untrue or not intended to be shared.

If you tend to be messy with your room, try to develop habits such as wiping down counters after you pour yourself some milk or make dinner.

Step 5 - Be Persistent and Monitor Your Progress

Persistency and consistency are two crucial factors to break a bad habit. You will never achieve your goal of changing your ways if you work hard for the first week only to dwindle your determination after several days. You should persistently on the go and keep track of your habits.

Breaking a bad habit, especially if you have had it years already, may never be easy. It is just natural to feel the urge just to give up. However, you must instill in your mind that giving up will not help you. Try focusing on the reward for all your hard work - better health, becoming more productive, or earning more money. Maintain your habit journal and be mindful of the moments when you catch yourself doing the habit again.

Step 6 - Cope with Setbacks

There is no magical formula that you can follow or a potion you can drink to completely remove a bad habit. Behaviors that you have learned for many years have the tendency to pop their ugly heads until you have completely broken them off. Because habits are fairly automatic, they could re-emerge anytime. Hence, you must develop the mindfulness (more on this in later chapters) and willpower to break these habits completely to avoid re-emergence. When you experience some lapses, try to find out why it has happened and continue making your efforts to be successful. The more your work on it, the higher the chance of your habit to break off.

It is also helpful if you start changing smaller bad habits (going back to sleep after the alarm sounds off, nail biting) so you can progress with major bad habits (procrastination, lying, taking too much debt). Once you have dealt with your smaller bad habits, you will be more inclined to take bigger challenges head-on.

Through CBT, you can effectively break the habit, and you can have a better chance to reduce your anxiety, increase your self-confidence, and live a better life. Bad habits are the precursor to addiction such as drug abuse, drinking, or smoking. Changing your bad habits will allow you to take care of yourself and your family.

It is crucial to be mindful of your bad habits such as tapping, nail biting, facial grimaces, twitching, repetitive mannerisms, and obsessional thinking. Most of these bad habits are caused by timidity, passivity, repressed anger, unresolved conflict, depression, cumulative stress, and internal tensions.

Chapter 5: Identify and Break Negative Thought Patterns

Getting rid of negative thinking and anxiety is easier said than done. As a matter of fact, studies reveal that even if you tell people to avoid thinking too much about a specific topic, it makes it even more difficult to get the thought pattern out of their minds.

However, indulging in negative thinking and re-running thoughts over and over in your head could be counterproductive and uncomfortable. In some instances, it could even result in chronic depression.

CBT can help you get away from staying too much on negative thinking by refocusing your mind on something positive. Through a series of therapy sessions, anyone who is heavily affected by negative thinking can benefit from rewiring the brain.

Most people who experience anxiety or depression caused by negative thinking should try CBT so the issues can be addressed immediately. Studies suggest that people who are depressed don't usually respond well to self-help techniques. Hence, it is recommended to attend CBT sessions for at least six weeks. A CBT specialist can teach you certain techniques that could help in counteracting the negative thought patterns associated with depression.

Common CBT Strategies to Help You Manage Negative Thinking

Identify the Root Problem that Causes Negative Thinking

It is important to find the problem and brainstorm for possible solutions. Talking with a psychotherapist and keeping a journal could help in discovering the root of negative thinking.

Write down every idea you have in mind. Think about the things that are bothering you and find ways to address the problem. Hopelessness is a trademark of depression. This is the belief that nothing can be better. Making a list of things that you can do to improve your current situation could help you to reduce the uncomfortable feeling.

For instance, if you are combating depression, there are many things you can do such as adopting a pet, signing up for a local club based on your interest, volunteering to a charity you care for and a lot more to avoid sinking further and deeper into it.

Keep a Journal to Help You Fight Negative Thinking

After determining triggers and aggravating factors for your depression, the next step is to be vigilant about the bad thoughts that often pop into your head to overpower the positive ones.

In your journal, try writing a self-statement to fight every negative thought. Take note of your self-statements and read them to yourself whenever you are being pulled down by your negative thoughts. As you go along with this discipline, you will eventually develop new associations that will replace negative thinking with positive ones.

But you should remember that self-statement must not be too far from negative thoughts as the mind might not be able to accept it. For instance, when the negative thought is "I'm so sad today" you should not try to fight it with. "I am really happy today." That would just be a complete lie. A better self-statement will be, *"It's okay to be sad. This is just an emotion. This too shall pass. And tomorrow will be a better day."*

This statement implies that it is fine to bump up the level of joy you may feel, and your mind will be in check to safeguard you from disappointment. It is healthy to recognize the part of our body and mind that are trying to help us cope with negative emotions.

Learn to Accept Disappointments

It is crucial to accept disappointment as part of our lives. The way we respond could affect how easily we can move forward. A teenager who is going through a bad breakup may blame trivial things such as simple acne, thinking, "There is no point in trying to look good. No one will like me."

A better approach is to allow yourself to experience disappointment and be reminded that there are things that are beyond our control. Focus instead on the things that you can control.

Take note of the details of your current situation, the lessons you have learned from the experience, and what you could do differently next time. This could help you move forward and be more positive about your future.

Look for Fresh Opportunities for Positive Thinking

Even those who enter a room and instantly think that they hate the furniture can probably rewire their brain to find at least three things in the room that they like. One easy technique is to set a phone reminder at least three times a day to rewire your thoughts for positive thinking. If you have a family or friend who also needs to manage their negative thinking, you can choose to buddy up and watch each other. This way, your team can share your thoughts and experiences.

The 3-Step CBT Technique of Challenging Your Thoughts

Cognitive restructuring - also known as thought challenging - is a CBT process wherein you need to challenge your negative thoughts that will only feed your anxiety, and instead of replacing them with more realistic and positive thoughts. This process involves three specific steps:

Step 1 - Identify Your Negative Thoughts

People who suffer from anxiety disorder perceive situations as more harmful than they really are. For example, for someone with a fear of germs, shaking hands is perceived as a high-risk activity. Even though this is often seen as an irrational fear, understanding these thinking patterns could be a challenge.

One way to workaround is to continue asking yourself what you were thinking when you began feeling anxious. Your CBT specialist can assist you in completing this step.

Step 2 - Challenge Negative Thinking

Next, your CBT specialist will assist you to effectively assess your thoughts that are causing your anxiety problem. This may include scrutinizing the validity of your worrisome thoughts, evaluating beliefs that are not helpful, and checking out the reality of negative predictions. The most common approaches for challenging negative thinking involve thinking about the real changes that what you are worried about may not really happen, comparing the advantages and disadvantages of anxiety, performing experiments, or avoiding the root cause of your fear.

Step 3 - Replace Negative Thinking with Realistic Thinking

After successfully identifying the negative distortions and irrational predictions in your negative thoughts, the next step is to replace them with fresh thoughts that are more positive and realistic. Your CBT specialist can also assist you in coming up with more accurate and relaxing statements that you can repeat to yourself when you are about to experience a situation that will usually cause you anxiety.

To better understand the mechanism of challenging your negative thoughts in CBT, let's examine this short example:

Betty doesn't want to keep jogging because she's worried about how she looks when she runs, and she thinks that everyone would laugh at her. Her CBT specialist asked her to make a list of her negative thoughts, figure out cognitive distortions, and work around with a more logical statement. Take a look at the results:

Negative Thought No. 1: What if I look silly when I go jogging?

Negative Distortion: Thinking about the worst case scenario

More Realistic Thought: No one ever told me I look silly.

Negative Thought No. 2: If I look silly, it will be terrible!

Negative Distortion: Blowing things out of proportion

More Realistic Thought: I am doing this for my health. That is not terrible.

Negative Thought No. 3: People might laugh at me

Negative Distortion: Jumping to conclusions

More Realistic Thought: Other people's opinion is none of my business

Certainly, it can be challenging to replace negative thoughts with more realistic ways of thinking. More often than not, negative thoughts have been part of our personalities for a long period of time. It usually takes time and effort to change this habit. This is why CBT also covers steps that you can do at home such as learning how you can recognize if you are worried and what it feels like physically and learning relaxation techniques and coping skills to combat panic and anxiety.

Exposure Therapy for Anxiety Disorder

We tend to avoid anxiety because it is rather unpleasant. Among the most common ways, people do this is by avoiding certain situations that make them feel anxious.

Chapter 6: Dealing with Panic Attacks

Have you ever feel a sudden surge of fear and overwhelming anxiety? If so, then you have experienced the feeling of a panic attack. You cannot breathe normally, your heart is pounding fast, and sometimes it feels like you are going crazy or dying. If a panic attack is not treated, one might be at the risk of developing a panic disorder. In fact, panic attacks can make you withdraw from normal activities. However, panic attacks can be treated and the sooner you seek help, the better. The right treatment and self-help plan can help you reduce and eventually eliminate the symptoms of panic. You will be able to regain your confidence and control your life.

A panic attack is defined as an intense flow of fear characterized by unexpected, debilitating and immobilizing intensity. These attacks often occur out of the blue, sometimes without a trigger or a warning. They can even attack you while you sleep or relax. For some people, a panic attack will be a onetime occurrence, but most people experience repeated episodes. In most cases, recurring panic attacks are triggered by a particular situation. For instance, a person may have a fear of speaking in public or crossing a bridge, especially if he/she had a panic attack from the same, previoously. Usually, a panic triggering situation is that which you feel endangered and probably unable to escape, thus triggering the body into fight or flight mode.

You may be perfectly happy and healthy and still experience one or two panic attacks. Also, our panic attacks may occur as part of other disorders such as social phobia, panic disorder, or depression. Panic attacks are treatable regardless of the cause. There are strategies one can use to deal with the symptoms and treat panic attacks.

Basically, the signs and symptoms of panic attacks occur very abruptly and can reach the peak within ten minutes. These symptoms will ,in most cases, end within 20 – 30 minutes and rarely last more than one hour. Panic attacks can happen anywhere at any time. They can attack you while you are walking down a street, shopping, driving, sleeping or even resting on a couch at home.

The symptoms of panic attacks include: shortness of breath, chest pain and discomfort, racing heart or palpitations, shaking or trembling, hyperventilation, feeling unreal or detached, nausea, upset stomach, sweating, hot/cold flashes, feeling dizzy, faint or lightheaded, losing control, tingling sensation, numbness, fear of dying or feeling of going crazy.

Note

In most cases, the symptoms of a panic attack are similar to those of a heart attack. In fact, many people make endless trips to the doctor thinking that they are dying. They find the symptoms so life-threatening that they head to the emergency room for medical care. Agreeably, it is important for a person to rule out possible medical issues that cause the same symptoms like panic attacks. One should not overlook panic as a potential cause of these symptoms.

Panic Disorders

While the majority of people develop just one or two panic attacks without much complications or disorders, there are others who experience more attacks developing into panic disorders. If you are the kind of experiencing one or two panic attacks, there is nothing to worry about. However, people with panic disorders should seek help. A panic attack is characterized by repetitive panic attacks leading to major changes in behavior and in some cases, persistent anxiety.

You may have panic disorders if you:

- ❖ Have been behaving differently because of attacks
- ❖ Have been experiencing frequent and unexpected panic attacks unrelated to any specific situation.
- ❖ Have been avoiding places and activities because you had a (previous attack)
- ❖ Are worrying a lot about having another attack

Although a panic attack has a short lifespan, the effects of the experience last longer, leaving an imprint. If you have a panic disorder, the attacks leave a bigger impact and emotional toll. Your confidence will be affected by the terror and intense fear that you felt during the panic attacks. These impacts can affect your daily routine greatly.

Eventually, you suffer from the following panic attack symptoms

- ❖ Phobic avoidance - This involves one avoiding certain environments and situations. A person may avoid these situations based on the false belief that the avoided situation caused the previous panic attacks. He/she may also avoid places where escape is difficult or unavailable in the event of an attack. When phobic avoidance goes to these heights, it is referred to as agoraphobia.

❖ Anticipatory anxiety – this involves feeling anxious and tensed in between panics instead of feeling relaxed and normal. This anxiety grows from the fear of having panic attacks in the future. This fear of panic becomes present most of the time, and it becomes very disabling.

What about **agoraphobia**?

Traditionally, agoraphobia was defined as the fear of open spaces or public places. However, recent researches have led to the thought that agoraphobia results from panic disorders and panic attacks. Although agoraphobia appears in the first year of panic attacks, it can develop at any time. Basically, if you are agoraphobic, then you are afraid of experiencing a panic attack in a situation where escape is embarrassing or difficult. You may also feel afraid of getting attacks when you cannot get help. These fears make you start avoiding more situations in life. For instance, you may begin to avoid:

- cars, planes, trains, subways et cetera
- Crowded places
- Social gatherings, meetings and other places where you would feel embarrassed if a panic attack occurred
- Crowded places such as shopping malls
- Foods and drinks that might change your [patterns such as alcohol, sugar, caffeine
- Certain medications
- Some physical exercises

↓ Going places without a person that makes you feel safe.

Causes of panic attacks and disorders

The causes of panic attacks and disorders have not been identified clearly yet, but researches show that the conditions run in families. Some studies have also found that there seems to be a relation between big life transformations and the condition. Examples of possible life transformation include graduating, entering a new workplace, having a baby, getting married, et cetera. Severe stress has also been linked to panic attacks. Besides, panic attacks can also result from medical conditions or certain physical causes. If you are having symptoms of panic attacks, it is important for you to visit a doctor to rule out the following possibilities; Hyperthyroidism, Mitral valve prolapse, hypoglycemia, Medication withdrawal, and Stimulant use.

Risk factors

Researches show that symptoms of panic disorder often begin in the late teenage years and early adulthood. It also affects more women than men. Some of the factors that might increase the risk of getting panic attacks and disorders include;

* Major life stress such as serious illness or the death of a loved one
* Family history of panic attacks and disorders
* Major changes in your life such as the addition of a baby or divorce

- ❖ Traumatic events such as a severe accident or sexual assault
- ❖ Excessive caffeine intake or smoking
- ❖ History of childhood abuse.

If left untreated, panic attacks and disorders can affect many areas in your life. You may find that fear of panic attacks makes you stay in constant stress, thus ruining the quality of your life. Some of the complications that might occur include:

- ❖ Development of certain phobias, for instance, the fear of leaving your home or driving
- ❖ Avoidance of social situations
- ❖ Frequent medical care for medical and health concerns
- ❖ Increased risk of suicidal thoughts and suicide
- ❖ Depression, anxiety disorders among others
- ❖ Alcohol and other substance abuse
- ❖ Financial challenges

It is important to note that panic attacks are not anxiety attacks even though people use the word interchangeably. These two words represent different experiences. The term panic attack describes the features of panic disorders and attacks occurring as a consequence of another mental disorder.

On the other hand, the term anxiety is used to outline the core features of different anxiety disorders. The collection of symptoms occurring as a result of being anxious (In a state of anxiety), for instance, shortness of breath, restlessness, difficulties concentrating, increased heartbeat, and restlessness may feel like an attack. However, these symptoms are not as heightened as those of a panic attack.

Prevention

Currently, there is no sure way of preventing panic attacks and disorders. However, you will need to

Seek treatment as soon as possible if you have these attacks

Follow the treatment plan so that the condition does not worsen or relapse,

Get regular physical activity – to help protect against anxiety.

No matter how helpless and powerless you feel when having a panic attack, you should know that there are things you can do help deal with the situation. Some of the exercises you can do to help overcome the panic include:

i.   Learn about panic attacks and disorders. – Having some knowledge about panic attacks can be empowering, thus relieving your distress. Do some research on panic disorders, distress, anxiety and the F3 response (Fight flight freeze). You will realize that the feelings you get when having a panic attack are normal and you are not alone. There are many articles and materials online.

ii. Learn and practice controlling your breathing. During a panic attack, hyperventilation brings on a variety of sensations such as chest tightness and lightheadedness. The relief for such a sensation and other panic symptoms is deep breathing. By learning how to control breath, you can counter the feelings of anxiety and panic as soon as they arise. Learning the breath control technique will ensure that you deal with the sensations scaring you.

iii. Avoid alcohol, smoking, and caffeine – for people who are susceptible to panic attacks, these substances can provoke the attacks. It is also important to watch out for medication containing stimulants such as diet pills.

iv. Practice relaxation techniques - some exercises such as meditation, progressive muscle relaxation and yoga can help your body to adapt relaxation. When practiced regularly, these practices help to respond to panic and anxiety. Besides, these practices increase good feelings, such as equanimity and joy.

v. Exercise regularly - One of the most natural relievers of anxiety is exercise; therefore, get moving. Rhythmic aerobic activities such as walking, swimming, running, and dancing can be very effective.

vi. Connect with family and friends. Panic attacks and anxiety can get worse if one feels isolated. It is important to connect with loved ones. If possible, make regular face to face connections. Explore ways to make new friends and build a support system.

vii. Get enough rest – Sometimes, poor sleep quality and insufficient rest can trigger anxiety or make it worse. Try to get as much rest as you can. If sleeping is a problem, look for guidelines on how to get a good night's sleep.

The most effective professional treatment for treating panic attacks, panic disorders and also agoraphobia is therapy. Cognitive behavioral therapy helps people to analyze their thinking patterns and behavior arising from their thoughts. In the case of panic attacks, the therapy helps one to look at the fears and their triggers in a more realistic way. For example, if you had an attack while driving, could you die? No. You might have to pull over to the, but it is very unlikely that you will crash into another car and die or have a heart attack. Once you realize that nothing extremely disastrous will happen, the thought of a panic attack becomes less terrifying.

Another exercise in cognitive behavioral therapy that helps one to tackle the panic attacks and anxiety is exposure therapy. This exercise allows you to be in the same environment as that you are afraid of but in a safe and controlled environment. It allows you to learn a healthy way to cope with whatever situation. You are asked to shake your head from side to side, hyperventilate or hold your breath so that the sensation of panic may reoccur. With each exposure, you will become less afraid of the strange bodily sensation felt during an attack and over time, you feel in control of the attacks.

Relaxation training is also used in many cases to help a person have better control of panic attacks. It is mostly applied in the initial stages of the treatment. In most cases, a person becomes so tensed and stressed because of the attacks that he /she forgets how to relax. The tension in the muscles makes them more susceptible to anxiety and panic attacks. Usually, relaxation techniques involve breathing and allowing the muscles to relax progressively. Relaxation counters the anxious physiological arousal and helps to reduce the risk of future attacks.

Chapter 7: Identify Assumptions and Core Beliefs

The Relational Frame Theory (RFT) frames the fundamental concept of ACT. RFT aims to explore the link between behavior and human language.

Understanding language is crucial in psychotherapy. Many of us use language in private when we think or in public when we speak with the people around us. We use language to think about, read about, write about, talk about, evaluate, relate, categorize, and describe everything around us.

Language is a useful tool in our existence as human beings, and without it, we may never had the chance to build our civilizations. For example, without language, we cannot develop laws and societal rules to regulate our behavior.

While human language offers a lot of benefits, it could also have negative aspects. It's like the yin and yang - it has a powerful dark side and the powerful bright side. And based on RFT, language plays a critical role in human suffering. Language is a tool we use to form prejudiced and hateful assumptions about people around us, construct negative thoughts, obsess over things, and revisit events that caused us trauma in the past. Too much use of language and thinking could also make it hard to keep in touch with the present moment. We could spend so much time thinking about our past and worrying about our future that we end up being unable to enjoy the present.

Through a deeper understanding of human language and its mechanism, we can better harness its bright side to minimize the effects of the dark side. This form of understanding is what RFT is trying to provide through ACT.

Psychotherapists who are studying how human language affects our behavior usually concentrate on two remarkable aspects of language: generativity and symbolism.

It is easy to understand symbolism as language is used to refer to an object or an idea. For example, the word "tree" refers to a type of plant with a trunk that supports branches, leaves, and may or may not bear flowers or fruits. Language is used to symbolize things. When you gain a better understanding of a specific word, then you can understand its meaning.

Meanwhile, generativity refers to our ability to create and understand an endless number of sentences with meaning. It is also known as productivity. Every language has a specific number of basic letters, sounds, and words. However, each one of us can produce an endless number of totally unique sentences with these words, letters, and sounds.

Various theories have been developed to explore these features and usually describe important properties or concentrate on various concerns. For instance, linguists believe that the novelty and complexity and generativity of language are mainly due to genetic factors. However, cognitive psychologists believe that our brain is responsible for how we process and store information, including symbolisms.

In spite of the differences in focus, most language studies are based on a similar idea that language is used to express information that is developed by our brains. Basically, language is a system of symbols that will allow us to express our ideas that can be understood by other people. These theories often concentrate on what are deemed to be the important processes of language.

Researchers and practitioners of RFT take a different method of exploring language and cognition. Instead of explaining language as a means of communicating ideas from one person to another, RFT focuses on how humans obtain language through interaction with people and their environment. This is framed to provide a useful and practical language analysis and cognition and not just a description of a concept.

ACT is considered as the applied technology of RFT as it tries to help people use language as a way to resolve specific psychological issues. This can be done through the psychological flexibility model that is distinct in ACT.

The Psychological Flexibility Model

The main objective in undergoing ACT is to enhance our psychological flexibility, which refers to our capacity to keep in touch with the present as a fully aware human being and depending on what the circumstances call for, persisting or changing in behavior to serve preferred values.

To put this simply, this means taking our own emotions and thoughts a bit more lightly, and behaving on long-term values instead of momentary feelings and thoughts, and impulses.

This could happen because emotions and thoughts tend to be shaky indicators for long-term values. It's not easy to control them, and they have the tendency to go to extremes. When we always allow our emotions and thoughts to influence our behavior, we might overlook the more significant, emerging trends of action and fail to grasp the genuine meaning in our lives, or experience life's richness.

At present, psychological flexibility is measured through the Acceptance and Action Questionnaire, which is used by psychotherapists and ACT specialists to predict the following psychological concerns:

- Depression
- Poor work performance
- Substance abuse
- Anxiety sensitivity
- Long-term disability
- Higher anxiety

- General pathology
- Alexithymia
- Worry

There are six fundamental ACT processes that establish psychological flexibility, and these will be discussed in detail in the next chapter. Take note that each process is considered as a positive psychological skill and not a special technique to resolve psychological concerns.

Chapter 8: Maintain Mindfulness

Mindfulness is a basic technique in psychotherapy that is used to mainly treat anxiety, anger, depression, and other psychological problems. While it has its roots in the mysticism of the Eastern cultures, science has already studied the subject a great deal and psychotherapists even recommend mindfulness meditation for individuals who are suffering from certain mental health problems. Developing mindfulness is a crucial part of CBT, as well as DBT and ACT. In fact, it is one of the four skills modules in DBT.

Basically, mindfulness is the state of our mind that can be achieved by focusing our awareness on what is happening at the present. It also involves the calm acceptance of our feelings, sensations, and thoughts.

The challenge of focusing in the present could be trivial for some, but this is actually easier said than done. Our mind could wander away, we lose touch with the present moment, and we could even be absorbed into obsessive thoughts about the things that have happened in the past or worrying about the future. But regardless of how far away our mind drifts away from the present, we can use mindfulness to immediately get us back to what we are presently doing or feeling.

Even though it is natural for us to be mindful anytime we want, we can cultivate it through effective ACT techniques that you will learn later on.

Mindfulness is usually linked with meditation. While meditation is an effective way to achieve mindfulness, there's more to it. Mindfulness is a form of being present, which you can use any time. It is a form of consciousness that you can achieve if you intentionally focus on the present moment without any judgment.

Elements of mindfulness

Attention and attitude are the two primary elements of mindfulness.

Attention

Many of us are suffering from what is known as the monkey mind, wherein the mind behaves like a monkey swinging from one branch to another. Our minds could swing away there and back again, and we usually don't have any idea how we end up thinking about something.

The monkey mind usually dwells in the past, ruminating what has happened or what you think must have happened if you have acted differently. It also swings away to the future, being anxious about what could happen. Nourishing the monkey mind will steal away the experience of the present moment.

Remember, mindfulness is focusing your attention on what is happening now.

Attitude

Suspending judgment and kindness are the basic tenets of mindfulness. Hence, a genuinely mindful person knows how to accept reality and doesn't engage in arguing with it. This may seem an easy task, but once you begin practicing mindfulness, you will be aware of how frequently we judge ourselves and our thoughts.

Here are some examples of sentences used in judgment of ourselves and others:

- I'm not good at this task.
- My shirt looks lame.
- I don't like my home.
- I really don't like my neighbor.
- What a grumpy waitress.

Mindfulness is also the art of calming our inner judge. It allows us to erase our internal expectations and become more embracing of how things are in the present moment. But take note that this doesn't mean you don't need to make necessary changes, and you will just allow everything to happen.

Remember, you are only suspending your judgment, so you can have more time to think about the situation and do something about it. The main difference is that you can make changes from the ideal state of your mind for change and not during times that you are influenced by tension or stress.

Moreover, mindfulness will allow you to be more compassionate with yourself, more embracing of your experience, and more caring of the people around you. It will also allow you to be more patient and non-judgmental if you make some lapses. As you practice mindfulness, you can reshape your brain to become kinder and more compassionate.

How Mindfulness Can Reshape Your Brain

In the past, people believed that the human brain could only be developed at a certain level, usually from early childhood to adolescence. But various studies reveal that our brain has the capacity to reorganize itself through forming neural connections. This is known as neuroplasticity, and it has no virtually no limit.

Neuroscientists shattered the old belief that the human brain is an unchanging, static organ. They discovered that despite of age, disease, or injury, the human brain can compensate for any damage by restructuring itself. To put it simply, our brain is capable of repairing itself.

More studies also support the idea that mindfulness can significantly help in the brain's development. It specifically helps in the process of neuroplasticity. It is really amazing to know that we can change our emotions, feelings, and thought processes through neuroplasticity and mindfulness.

There are three major studies that show how mindfulness can rewire the human brain through neuroplasticity.

Mindfulness Can Improve Memory, Learning, and Other Cognitive Functions

Even though mindfulness meditation is linked with a sense of physical relaxation and calmness, practitioners claim that the practice can also help in learning and memory.

Sara Lazar, a professor at Harvard University Medical School, pioneered an 8-week meditation program that primarily uses mindfulness. With her team of researchers from Massachusetts General Hospital, she conducted the program to explore the connection between mindfulness and the improvement of cognitive functions.

The program was composed of weekly meditation sessions as well as audio recordings for the 16 volunteers who practiced meditation alone. On average, the participants practiced meditation for around 27 minutes. The underlying concept of the mindfulness meditation for the research was on achieving a state of mind in which the participants will suspend their judgment and just focus on feeling sensations.

Later on, the team used Magnetic Resonance Imaging (MRI) to capture images of the brain structure of the participants. A group of individuals who were not meditating (the control group) were also asked for MRI scan.

The researchers were amazed by the result. Primarily, the study participants revealed that they experienced significant cognitive advantages that were proven in their responses in the mindfulness survey. On top of that, the researchers also noted measurable physical differences in the density of the gray matter as supported by MRI scan.

- The gray-matter density in the amygdala, the area of the brain responsible for stress and anxiety was decreased.
- There were significant changes in the brain areas responsible for self-awareness, introspection, and compassion
- The gray-matter density in the hippocampus, the part of the brain responsible for memory and learning was increased.

This Harvard study reveals that the brain's neuroplasticity, and through practicing meditation, we can play an active role in the development of our brain. It is exciting to know that we can do something every day to improve our quality of life and general well-being.

Mindfulness Can Help Combat Depression

Millions of people around the world are suffering from depression. For example, in the US, there are about 19 million people who are seeking medication to combat depression. This is around 10% of the whole US population.

Dr. Zindel Segal, a Psychiatry Professor at the University of Toronto used a research grant from MacArthur Foundation to explore the advantages of mindfulness towards alleviating depression. The research that was mainly focused on the administration of Mindfulness Based Stress Reduction session was considered a success that he conducted a follow-up research to study the effectiveness of mindfulness meditation to patients afflicted by depression. This has resulted in the establishment of Mindfulness Based Cognitive Therapy or MBCT.

The study involved patients who are suffering from depression, with 8 out of 10 experiencing at least three episodes of depression. Meanwhile, around 30% of the study participants who experienced at least three episodes of depression had not relapsed for more than a year in comparison to those who followed a prescribed therapy (mainly through antidepressants).

The result was astounding that it has become a precursor of several research sponsored by the Oxford and Cambridge University in the United Kingdom, with both studies generating similar outcomes. The research has significantly proved valuable in using mindfulness meditation as an effective and healthier alternative to medication in the UK that has convinced mental health practitioners to prescribe mindfulness meditation to their patients.

Mindfulness meditation and research studies on MBCT are gradually taking a foothold within medical and scientific circles in the US and other parts of the globe.

Mindfulness Can Help in Stress Relief

A study conducted at the Carnegie Mellon University has revealed that the practice of mindfulness, even for 25 minutes a day, can alleviate stress. The study, led by Prof. David Creswell, involved 66 participants with ages between 18 and 30 years.

More important, with being mindful, we also get to experience life more fully.

Mindfulness skills also train our minds, and so we get the added benefits of improved memory, sharper focus, and faster mental processing. Our anxiety is also reduced, and we gain more control over our thoughts.

Core Mindfulness Skills

And so, what exactly are these mindfulness skills? They are divided into three groups: Wise Mind, the "what" skills, and the "how" skills.

Wise Mind

As explained above, this is the middle state between our Reasonable Mind and Emotion Mind, where we recognize both our reason and emotions, and act accordingly.

The "What" Skills

These skills are in answer to the question, "What are the things you must do to practice mindfulness?" The answers are (1) to observe, (2) to describe, and (3) to participate.

Observe.

To observe is nothing more than to experience and be aware of our surroundings, our thoughts, our feelings, and the sensations we're receiving. This is stepping back and looking at ourselves, especially for reorientation, when we are too much preoccupied with our problems.

Describe.

To describe is to put words on our present experiences — acknowledging what we feel, think, or do — and using only the facts to do it, without our own opinions. For example, we say to ourselves, "My stomach feels hungry," or "I'm thinking about my mother." Doing this lessens distraction and helps our focus.

Participate.

To participate is to give ourselves fully to what we are doing at the moment (eating, talking, or feeling satisfied). We forget ourselves in it, and we act spontaneously.

The "How" Skills

These skills, on the other hand, answer the question, "How are you going to practice mindfulness?" The answers are: (1) non-judgmentally, (2) one-mindfully, and (3) effectively.

Non-judgmentally. A nonjudgmental stance is seeing only the facts without evaluating, and without personal opinion. We accept each moment as it is, including our circumstances and what we see in ourselves: our thoughts, our feelings, our values, etc.

Chapter 9: Work through Worry, Fear, and anxiety

An anxiety attack happens when an individual gets an episode of intense fear or panic. Expectedly, anxiety attacks happen fast and without warning. In some cases, there is a known trigger, such as getting stuck in an elevator or thinking about making a speech to a large audience, but in other cases, the attacks happen with little anticipation. The anxiety attacks tend to peak within ten minutes and rarely last for more than thirty minutes. During this period of an anxiety attack, the victim will experience terror and feel overwhelmed or feel as if they are about to die. Relatedly, the clinical manifestation of anxiety attacks is highly frightening that most people think that they have a heart attack. When the anxiety attack is over, the affected person may worry about getting another one, especially in a public place where help is not easily available or where one cannot escape easily.

Correspondingly, the symptoms of an anxiety attack include feeling a surge of overwhelming panic, hyperventilation, feeling of losing control, feeling like you are passing out, nausea, feeling detached, shaking, or chills. One should seek intervention if you start avoiding certain situations due to being afraid of having a panic attack. Fortunately, panic attacks are highly manageable. In most cases, most people are free of panic attacks within just five to eight treatment sessions.

Furthermore, people with social anxiety attacks display fear and avoidance as a way of coping with future attacks. All these developments relate to a panic disorder that can happen with or without agoraphobia. People that have experienced anxiety attacks will show fear of experiencing panic attack symptoms in contexts that feel either emotionally embarrassing or physically difficult to escape from. Most people with anxiety attacks fear the physical symptoms of panic attacks due to the belief that they may have an underlying medical issue which aggravates the worry. Such people may feel at ease from these attacks by remaining within certain areas or a premeditated safe zone without experiencing intense fear. When the person can no longer leave the defined physical safe zone without showing intense fear, then the person is considered as having agoraphobia.

Additionally, anxiety attacks are recurrent, implying that they will happen multiple times without warning. The physical symptoms of an anxiety attack, such as difficulty breathing, shaking, and heart palpitations can make the individual feel that they are in grave danger. Some people with anxiety attacks feel as if they are going insane. Some of the physical symptoms of panic attacks are akin to those of social anxiety disorder such as excessive sweating and shaking.

Unlike social anxiety disorder, individuals may experience anxiety attacks that may seem comfortable engaging in social interactions. Like those with social anxiety disorder, people with anxiety attacks feel embarrassed about having others see them have a panic attack. For this reason, a trusted family member or friend can help support a loved one with an anxiety attack. Most people with panic disorders enjoy social interactions and can benefit from social support but the attempt to keep the panic a secret makes such people suffer loneliness. Similarly, individuals with social anxiety disorder experience high levels of loneliness even though such people may want to socialize with others; the anxiety is highly overwhelming.

Causes of anxiety attacks

Even though the specific causes of anxiety attacks are relatively known, the disorder tends to run in families. Major life transitions are known to trigger anxiety attacks, and they include graduating from college and joining the workplace or getting married. Death of a loved one severe cause stress, and so makes the loss of a job or divorce, which can trigger panic attacks. Additionally, such attacks can also be a manifestation of underlying medical conditions as well as other physical causes such as mitral valve prolapse which is a minor cardiac problem that occurs when one of the valves of the heart does not close correctly. An overactive thyroid gland known as hyperthyroidism can also trigger anxiety attacks symptoms. The other conditions include hypoglycemia, stimulant use, and medication withdrawal.

In overall, women are at more risk of developing anxiety attack compared to men. Anxiety commonly manifests when one feels overwhelmed, and some of the triggers include financial pressure, work pressure, family problems, separation, concerns about parenthood, challenges with coping with administrative issues, changing life situations, reduced mobility, loss of mental function and having a diagnosis of a chronic condition.

Additionally, an anxiety attack can be caused by several phobias other than a social phobia, genetic factors, changes in the brain, major stress, excessive stimulant use, use of certain medication, a history of substance use, the use of some medications, and a post-traumatic experience. As indicated anxiety is triggered by exposure to the feared situation or object that includes public speaking, exposure to a phobia, and a fear of having a panic attack.

Pathophysiology of anxiety attacks

Responses to anxiety are an adaptive response and prepare an individual for vigorous defensive action when there is a proximal predatory threat. When an anxiety attack happens, intense fear is aroused by sympathetic activity even when there is no actual danger. Most neuroendocrinological studies implicate dysfunction of the hypothalamic-pituitary-adrenal axis even though this disturbance happens later in the progression of the disorder after anticipatory anxiety development and associated distress. Issues with the normal functioning of the amygdala of the brain, hypothalamus, thalamus, and brain stem regions impact the development and progression of anxiety attacks.

Theories of anxiety attacks

Anxiety attacks due to the biological theory

Neurotransmitters send signals between various sites in the brain and tend to impact the mood and anxiety levels of a person. The imbalance of one or more neurotransmitters is thought to trigger anxiety, and this is the biological theory of anxiety. Anxiety in these cases happens due to erratic processing of normal fear as intense fear making the individual feel that they are in grave danger. The Gamma-aminobutyric acid reinforces the assumptions of the biological theory on what causes anxiety in human beings. As a brain in the brain, the gamma-aminobutyric acid modulates anxiety. The chemical, gamma-aminobutyric acid balances excitement in the human brain by mediating relaxation and depressing anxiety levels and recent studies suggest that gamma-aminobutyric acid may have an impact in most mental disorders such as mood disorders and anxiety. Most of the anti-anxiety medications target gamma-aminobutyric acid receptors in the brain, leading to a more composed and relaxed person. In some studies, the levels of gamma-aminobutyric acid in persons with anxiety attacks were significantly lower compared to individuals with no history of anxiety attacks.

Anxiety form a metabolic theory viewpoint

Most individuals with anxiety attacks show high sensitivity to certain substances compared to those without a history of anxiety attacks. For instance, some people experience anxiety attacks by receiving an injection of lactic acid that the body generates naturally during muscular activity. Some people will experience anxiety attacks by breathing air with elevated levels of carbon dioxide. For some people taking any stimulant such as caffeine will trigger anxiety. However, there is no consensus on causatives of anxiety as brain chemical messengers are interactive and complex. In overall, most people agree that anxiety attacks are caused by a variety of factors, including genetic and environmental influences.

What anxiety attacks are not

It is necessary to define the scope of anxiety attacks to avoid the unwarranted assumption that any form of anxiety episode is an anxiety attack. Such an attack is not necessarily a heart attack even though most clinical presentations may appear like those of a heart attack. Most people suffering from an anxiety attack make trips to the doctor, thinking that it is a life-threatening medical issue. Even though it is important to rule out any potential medical issue when chest pain, difficulty breathing, and elevated heart rate manifest, in some cases, it is just an anxiety attack.

Diagnosing an anxiety attack

A mental health professional can accurately determine the presence of an anxiety attack by diagnosing social anxiety disorder or a panic disorder. However, mental health professionals cannot directly diagnose an anxiety attack as it is not clinically specified in the DSM-5, which is a scientifically developed premise for defining and diagnosing mental health conditions. However, these health professionals can recognize anxiety attacks and the underlying mental health condition. Sometimes it might be necessary to rule out physiological conditions that show similar signs and symptoms.

Treating anxiety attacks

Just like the underlying mental health conditions, anxiety attacks are treated through therapy but can also be treated using pharmacological interventions. Through cognitive behavioral therapy, the focus is given to learning approaches and activities that fuel the anxiety attacks and helps the patient to examine their fears in a more pragmatic manner.

Additionally, there is exposure therapy for managing anxiety attacks by allowing the patient to navigate the physical sensations of panic in a safe and managed environment. All these developments give the individual an opportunity to create healthier ways of coping. One might be asked to hyperventilate, hold their breath, or shake their head from the side from to side. With each exposure, the patient will become less afraid of these internal bodily sensations and feel a greater sense of control over the panic.

Pharmacological interventions for anxiety attacks

As indicated, medications can be used to manage anxiety attacks for a short-term. These medicines do not resolve the underlying condition, and they should not be the only form of treatment available for the patient with anxiety attacks. For instance, the medication should be combined with lifestyle changes and therapy to help address the underlying problem. Some of these medications include antidepressants, and they may take weeks to start working and have to be taken continuously even when there is no anxiety attack happening. The other class of medication for anxiety attacks is benzodiazepines, which are anti-anxiety attacks drugs and act very quickly, usually within thirty minutes to an hour. Taking benzodiazepines during an anxiety attack can give fast relief of symptoms. Unfortunately, benzodiazepines are highly addictive and present serious withdrawal symptoms so they should be used cautiously

Helping someone with an anxiety attack

It is frightening to see a friend or someone close to you suffering from an anxiety attack. Usually, the breathing of such an individual becomes abnormally shallow and fast that the person becomes dizzy, trembles, sweats, feel nauseous, or thinks that they have a heart attack. Even though the individual response may seem irrational, it is important to view the world from the victim's eyes. A person suffering from anxiety attack thinks that the danger is real, and simply asking them to calm down helps a lot. Helping the affected person to navigate the panic attack is important to manage future attacks.

Additionally, act calm as being composed and understanding, as well as non-judgmental, will help the affected person's anxiety to subside normally. There are situations where a person close to the victim of anxiety also attacks panic, which tends to worsen the anxiety or post-anxiety recovery of the victim. Think of a friend of a person suffering from an anxiety attack, and the friend starts screaming that the person has a heart attack which only reinforces the anxiety of the victim.

Furthermore, learn about panic and anxiety if you have a friend with anxiety attacks. By knowing about anxiety, you will assist the friend with anxiety attacks to understand them and think of overcoming them. As with any other mental condition, there are higher chances of making the treatment effect if the patient is the one who asked for the treatment. Close friends are important in providing an understanding and supportive environment for the patient. In most cases, we assume knowledge of mental health aspects when, in reality, we know not. For instance, most people assume they understand what emotions are, but the reality is that they do not.

It is also important for the person with an anxiety attack to shin alcohol, caffeine, and smoking as all these provoke anxiety attacks in vulnerable people. Unfortunately, quitting the usage of some of these stimulants and drinks require an independent therapy, but they are manageable. Another common mistake that individuals with anxiety attacks make is that they might resort to drinking or smoking to escape from the fear of anxiety attacks or to lessen anticipated anxiety attack.

Additionally, one should learn to manage their breathing as hyperventilation brings on many sensations, including feeling chest tightness and lightheadedness that manifest during anxiety attacks. Fortunately, deep breathing can relieve most of these symptoms. When one learns to control their breathing, then they will manage to calm themselves down when they begin to feel anxious.

Correspondingly, practice relaxation techniques such as yoga, progressive muscle relaxation, and medication will strengthen the relaxation response of the body. The opposite of stress response involved in panic and anxiety is calming down of the body and feeling in control of everything. All these relaxation practices promote relaxation and also increase feelings of joy and equanimity. Anxiety makes the muscles and the entire body tense making the person feel like he or she does not exist. By learning to relax the mind and the body, the person with anxiety attacks may start to feel complete and in charge.

It is also important that one avoids isolation. Interacting with friends, face-to-face interaction will increase the emotional stamina and processing of fear for the affected individual. Interacting with friends physically may also serve as a limited form of exposure where the person gets to face their worst fears in small and mild forms. It might also become easier for the individual to recover from an anxiety attack when surrounded by friends.

Equally important is that one should get enough and quality sleep. An inadequate amount of sleep or poor quality of sleep will only worsen anxiety. Try getting at least six hours of uninterrupted sleep. While it might appear an easy exercise and process, most people have difficulties getting continuous quality sleep. Fortunately, they are several tips that can be found online on how to achieve quality uninterrupted sleep.

Tips for managing anxiety

Know the signs of anxiety. Unlike panic disorder and panic attacks, most anxiety attacks have a fairly predictable cause. When one knows the signs of anxiety, then he or she is likely to take action when the first few signs start manifesting. Some of the signs of anxiety attack may include overeating and inability to sleep.

Understand your triggers. The triggers of an anxiety attack vary from person to person, and one must learn to recognize what makes them feel anxious. For instance, taking a significant workload or asking someone for held may be part of the triggers that activate your anxiety. Once you identify the triggers, consider managing them.

It is also important to take diet into consideration as a busy lifestyle can lead to much fast food or limited exercise. Create time for getting a healthful meal or pack a home-made healthy meal to the office.

Learn to exercise as sitting for lengthy periods of time will worsen latent anxiety. Learn to take a 30-minute break and walk to enhance your well-being. The other advantage of exercising is that it helps convert emotional energy into physical energy, which relaxes the mind.

Commit to being social by spending time with friends and family. One can also look for another group other than family to interact with. By joining an emotional support group, one will learn to ease the mind off social anxieties.

It is also necessary that one sets goals. When feeling overwhelmed with administrative or financial problems, try to sit down and plan. Define targets and priorities and evaluate them off as you sort them out. Having a plan will help determine how much workload one can take.

Illustration of an anxiety attack

James is a 35-year old male, enters the emergency room after getting an episode of extreme chest pain, numbness in the arms, and difficulty breathing. James states the following to the physician:

"I was taking a walk with my pet dog when I began sweating. Since it was not hot outside, I could not understand why. Then I began having trouble breathing and really felt scared. I thought my heart would explode as it was pounding so hard. When my knees felt week, it seemed like my entire body was trembling, and then my arms went numb. I realized later that the whole episode lasted a few minutes, but it felt like each second was an hour. Am I going insane? Did I have a heart attack? I felt like I was going to die."

When James was given an electrocardiogram, the test comes back in the normal range, showing that he did not have a heart attack. The physician believes that James may have had a panic attack and referred him to a clinical psychologist.

After four weeks, James saw the psychologist and reported that he experienced over two-dozen anxiety attacks with similar symptoms since being taken to the emergency room. At this juncture, the daily productivity and social life of James were negatively impacted as he avoided going to work, having time with friends and family, and walking with his dog as he thinks that it might precipitate another attack. A deeper analysis shows that James has a social anxiety disorder as diagnosed by the psychologist.

Relatedly, the therapist gave James a biofeedback monitor that tracks his pulse and teaches him to breathe slowly and deeply to lower the heart rate. When James experiences an anxiety attack, he uses the machine to adjust his breathing until the machine light turns green which is an indicator that the heart rate of James is no longer dangerously elevated and signals the end of the anxiety attack. The therapist recommended this biofeedback monitor as it gives consistent, accurate information about heart rate over time.

What Leads to Social Anxiety?

Some studies argue that brain scans of individuals with social phobia show hyperactivity in the amygdala region of the brain. The amygdala region of the brain handles most of the physiological changes linked to the reaction. For instance, cognitive-behavioral therapy can help individuals with social anxiety adjust their brain processing of real and imagined fears. Additionally, researchers may look at the blood flow differences in specific areas of the brain for individuals struggling with extreme social phobia. The sites in the brain involved in anxiety are known. Extreme social anxiety happens when some of these sites in the brain continuously process fear and magnify the fear that is nonexistent, making the entire body captive of its thoughts. Using neuroimaging one study of blood flow in the brain determined the differences in the brains of individuals with a social anxiety disorder when speaking in public. It emerged that individuals with a social anxiety disorder had enhanced blood flow in their amygdala that is integral to the limbic system associated with fear. On the other hand, the neuroimaging of the brain of people with social anxiety indicated an enhanced flow of blood to the cerebral cortex, which is an area linked to thinking and evaluation. It appears that people with social anxiety condition have their brain reacting to social situations differently than people without the condition.

An individual with an anxiety condition is likely to have imbalances of certain chemicals in the brain known as neurotransmitters. The role of neurotransmitters is to signal one cell to the other cell. The neurotransmitters involved in anxiety include serotonin, norepinephrine, dopamine, and gamma-aminobutyric acid. Individuals with social anxiety disorder display some of the same issues of these neurotransmitters as individuals suffering from agoraphobia and panic disorder. The exact manner in which these chemicals influence social anxiety disorder is still under study.

Impact of parenting styles on social anxiety

The approach to parenting has a lasting impact on different aspects of a child's life, and these include psychological stability and well-being. Authoritative parents and perfectionist parents are likely to create an anxiety problem in their children in later life. Children that grew up under perfectionist parents may suffer self-esteem issues because the normal levels of accomplishment are regarded as average or failure, making one feels inadequate, and this can affect their social life.

Against this backdrop, one might feel not competent to contribute to groups, and this may make the individual fear facing people. People that had perfectionist and authoritative parents may feel that they are not just ready to engage in group work, or they might feel inadequate and fear meeting people and displaying their weakness. While this may also manifest in individuals without a history of anxiety attacks, for sufferers of anxiety, this feeling is intense and makes the person feels powerless.

Environmental factors that contribute to social anxiety disorder

Indeed the environment that one grows in affects their psychosocial competencies. For this reason, if any of your parents had social phobia, then chances are that you are likely to manifest it. Psychologists have created models that see to determine how children develop social anxiety through learning. Some of the assumed ways that children develop social anxiety include direct conditioning by subjecting the child to an early terror event that may have a lasting effect on the manifestation of social phobia later in the life of the child.

For instance, if other kids made fun of the child or if the child was constantly bullied are some of the experiences that precipitate social anxiety later in the life of that child.

Additionally, observing learning may contribute to a child developing a social anxiety disorder. For instance, the child may have observed a family member or a friend go through a traumatic social event, and this may have had some negative impact on the child. There is also information transfer where socially anxious and fearful parents unknowingly transfer verbal and non-verbal information to their children about the dangers of social situations. If the mother worries a lot about what other people think of her, then the child is likely to develop the same type of anxiety due to information transfer. In overall, the way a child is brought up can also affect the chances that the child will acquire a social anxiety disorder. Where one or both parents were rejecting, critical, controlling, and were not allowed developing appropriate social skills, then their child is at risk of developing a social anxiety disorder in later life.

Childhood behavioral inhibition causes of social anxiety disorder

At one point, you have met a child that easily upset. Such a child is likely to withdraw, cry, or seek the comfort of a parent when faced with these types of situations. Children that exhibit this type of behavior are showing behavioral inhibition. The persistent inability to process temper, negative emotions, and comprehend disappointment may signal a mental health issue. According to this view, people with anxiety could have developed during childhood. The implication of this finding is that early interventions are likely to enhance the positive outlook for individuals with a social anxiety condition. It appears that social phobia builds over childhood and manifests significantly when one is a young adult indicating that most parents tend to dismiss signs of anxiety in their children.

Some parents are likely to dismiss children as being clingy or feeling temperamental when separated briefly from caregivers. However, in line with this view, parents should watch out for children that overreact when separated from their caregivers.

Genetic causes of social anxiety disorder

There is new thinking that social phobia could be caused by a particular genetic composition that made the person prone to developing the disorder. People with a family member with a social anxiety disorder are two to six times more likely to develop the disorder. It is estimated that around 30% to 40% of social anxiety disorder sufferers also have it in their families, suggesting that it is the heritable condition. The remaining variation is thought to be caused by environmental factors. However, researchers have not established a specific genetic makeup linked to social anxiety disorder but have determined specific chromosomes associated with anxiety issues and disorders such as panic disorder and agoraphobia.

Societal causes of social anxiety disorder

Some cultures precipitate social phobias. Think of a culture that requires one to join and fit into society perfectly. Such a culture is likely to push one into uneasiness and extreme worry on whether he or she is up to the task. Some cultures demand collectiveness, which implies that one must fit and function well within groups. A child or a young adult in such a culture will be under intense pressure to fit into this preset societal structures.

Technological factors that cause extreme social anxiety

The Internet of Things has made the world to be one big virtual community, and we spend a significant portion of time interacting with us online but not physically. Social media, texting, and a library of applications allow us to communicate without physically meeting. There is an increasing amount of online content, video games, and shows that we consume instead of interacting with each other physically. Some therapists argue that spending a significant amount of time online rather than in physical world interactions precipitates one to anxiety when meeting real people because online provides the allure of anonymity making it easier for one to initiate a communication.

Correspondingly, there is clinical evidence indicating that there is a link between online communications and social anxiety. When more people switch to online communication, they are likely to miss out on frequent exposure to physical, social situations and associated learning of how to navigate them. Online space can be highly controllable and make an individual accustomed to positive communication, but real life is different as communication and feedback is dynamic. In one study by the University of California, it emerged that adolescents are comfortable with online communication and communication but anxious regarding in-person physical, social interaction.

Physical causes of anxiety condition

People that have social anxiety will have their anxiety triggered by physical events that include shortness of breath and these include leaving home, large crowds, interacting with others, moving, catching a judgmental look from someone, or situations where people might assess you. You will notice that the causes of social anxiety condition and social anxiety are the same as the social anxiety being the most severe, and as such, the causes are more intense and multi-layered. Think of someone that grew up in a mentally healthy environment and has a secure temperament. Such a person could have inherited some social anxiety from her mother, but the individual did not have any traumatic experiences that worsen it. Such an individual is likely not to develop a social anxiety condition. On the other hand, think of someone that has had an insecure attachment as a child and suffered abuse as well as bullying during teenage years. Additionally, the parents of the person have social anxiety and raised him in a manner that encourages socially anxious behavior. The person is likely to show social anxiety as opposed to social anxiety. For this reason, social anxiety condition causes significant distress and can stop an individual from having a normal life. As expected, social anxiety is easier to manage, and everyone processes a little social anxiety as they meet new people and make changes in their lives.

In overall, environmental and genetic factors contribute significantly to the development of social phobia. The environmental factors make one learn to think that people and social interactions are a danger to the person. In reaction, the individual spends significant time avoiding people or limiting the interaction. For some sufferers of anxiety, being in a social gathering may trigger an anxiety attack and make the person think that he or she will die. On the other hand, genetic makeup may make one susceptible to anxiety attacks even though the exact genetic role in mediating and moderating anxiety is under study.

i) Manage your breathing

Notably, anxiety causes changes in the body that can make one uncomfortable. For instance, anxiety can make your breathing fast and shallow, and this will make one more anxious. Individuals with anxiety may feel dizzy, tense, or suffocated. However, certain breathing techniques can help one slow the breathing and handle other anxiety symptoms. The benefit of the breathing exercise is that it can be done anywhere as well as during and after an episode of anxiety.

The justification for controlling breathing is that it can mediate and moderate anxiety. Breathing fast can trigger uneasiness and invite an anxiety attack. By managing to breathe through taking deep breaths, one learns to influence the body and the mind, and these are vital developments in managing social phobia. Think of how fast you breathe when feeling angry or anxious. Fortunately, breathing can be controlled easily, but it requires intense practice.

ii) Progressive muscle relaxation

Studies indicate that certain physical activities, such as jogging can help lower anxiety levels. Progressive muscle relaxation can help. Flexing and releasing groups of muscles in the body and maintaining your attention on the feeling of the release. Additionally, yoga can assist one to calm the muscles down. As indicated, certain types of breathing can help lower blood pressure and heart rate. Doing yoga for a few months can help ease overall anxiety.

iii)   Plan ahead for social situations

Planning ahead for social situations that make you nervous can enable you to feel more confident. If certain situations make you anxious, then you might feel the urge to shun such situations. However, by preparing for what you are anticipating can help improve your reaction to such events. For instance, try reading newspapers and magazines before going on a first date as it might make you scared, and with that preparation, you will get a few topics to talk about. Do some relaxation or breathing exercises if going to a party triggers symptoms to help you calm before you leave the house.

iv)   Start gradually

Avoid starting bug but start with small social situations. For instance, schedule restaurant meals with family or friends so you can get used to eating in public. Try to make eye contact with people on the street and greet them. If an individual starts a conversation with you ask them questions about their hobbies or favorite places to travel. With time you can navigate big social activities as you get more comfortable. Additionally, try to be patient with yourself as it takes time and practice to face social anxiety. It is not advisable to confront your biggest fears right away as taking up large challenges within a short period can trigger more anxiety.

v) Shift the focus from yourself

Start by shifting the attention from yourself to what is happening around you. Let go of the focus on what is in your head to what is happening around you. One way to attain this is to remain in the moment by listening to the current conversation rather than reflecting. Additionally, assure yourself that other people cannot tell how anxious you are by just taking a look at you. People appreciate when others act genuine and interested, and it helps to focus on the present and be a good listener.

vi)   Talk back to negative feelings

Negative thoughts may be about situations or people and may even occur automatically. In most cases, the thoughts that are negative are not justified, but they can make you misread things such as facial expressions. All these developments can make you think that people are talking about you. Using a pen and a piece of paper think of all the negative thoughts you have in specific situations. Then noted them and wrote down positive thoughts that challenge negative thoughts. For instance, a negative thought could be 'I am feeling anxious, and I will not manage to handle it". Then the challenge could be "I have felt anxious before, but I have always navigated through successfully, which means I will do my best to focus on the positive parts of the experience."

vii)   Listen to your senses

The senses of smell, taste, sight, touch, and sound can help calm you at the moment when you are feeling anxious. For some individuals, looking at a favorite photograph or smelling a particular scent can enable you to overcome the anxiety. The next moment you begin to feel anxious about a social situation, try to listen to your choice songs, snuggle with a pet, or chew a favorable piece of gum. Our senses are part of the emotional system as we sense and exhibit our feelings through the senses. For instance, when angry or restless and you touch a smooth, natural fur, there are chances that one will feel a calming effect. Additionally being in an environment with bright lights or flickering lights may aggravate anxious feelings. However, being in a room with a moderate amount of light can enhance the feeling of calmness. Avoid areas full of noise or loud music as these can worsen the anxiety.

viii) Take meals

Most people with anxiety disorders also skip meals, especially breakfast. Taking breakfast and other meals are necessary to sustain the energy levels throughout the day. Skipping a meal tends to create a spike in blood sugar and blood flow after the meal is taken, and this can heighten effects such as sweating and tiredness, which can trigger social anxiety. People with social anxiety fear to embarrass themselves or attracting attention, and sweating will make them think other people are noticing the uneasiness they are displaying. The meals taken should not trigger or worsen inflammation, as this would only make anxiety symptoms intense.

As expected, few people take the implication of proper meals seriously. Having the right meal at the right time helps ensure that the body is uniformly powered and experiences fewer diet-related inflammation. At one point, you might have felt awkward due to flatulence occasioned by the meal you took last night. Investing in a proper diet is important if one wants to lessen triggers of anxiety at a personal level.

ix)   Meditation

Notably, there is mindfulness meditation as a technique of mindfulness and relaxation. In this method, one sits comfortably and concentrates on breathing as well as inviting your attention to the mind to the current moment. The mind tends to wander into the past or future to help create continuity. Mindfulness meditation is likely to help individuals with depression, anxiety, and pain. The goal of this technique is to slow down the mind from being preoccupied with the future or the past. The mind controls us, but in mindfulness and relaxation techniques, we are trying to control it. Like any other form of meditation, one requires a calm place that is free from physical and electronic forms of distractions to successfully engage in mindfulness meditation.

x) Relaxation exercises

For instance, yoga is increasingly being used as a mindfulness and relaxation technique. Yoga entails a series of flowing movements where the physical aspects are expected to align with mental focus and distract the individual from continued thoughts. When feeling disturbed, it is a combination of emotional energy and physical energy that reinforce each other or rival each other, which wears us out. Through yoga, we harness both the physical and mental energy to calm the entire body. The other benefit of yoga is that it can improve flexibility and balance. In this way, yoga not only calms you but also exercise you. However, due to its physical cost to the body, yoga might be unfit for persons with certain health conditions. Therefore, yoga might be unreasonable to persons with pain or health problems that inhibit movements.

Techniques you can use to manage time

Some individuals feel unease if they have several commitments at once. Such commitments may include work, family, and health-linked activities. By having a plan in place for the next necessary action can aid in keeping this anxiety at bay. Through effective time management strategies, one can focus on one task at a time and not feel overwhelmed. They are numerous open-source online apps for managing workload and planning. For most people, breaking major projects into manageable modules makes it easy to manage and accomplish them effortlessly.

Even though it appears an easy undertaking, most individuals are poor time managers. Poor time management also implies interference with sleep duration and quality of sleep. Think of an individual who manages time poorly and takes supper at midnight. Due to late meals, the individual increases the risk of indigestion and acidity, and this makes the person struggle with getting quality and timely sleep. The individual then wakes up the following day, feeling not well rested and easily irritable. Additionally, the person does not feel highly confident, and this worsens the social phobia of the person.

i) Aromatherapy

Stress and anxiety can be eased through smelling soothing plant oils. As expected, different people prefer different scents, and experimenting is encouraged. However, it is important to take into consideration those with breathing difficulties and allergies when experimenting with scents as part of aromatherapy. Several studies suggest that aromatherapy may be helpful in easing anxiety.

While aromatherapy is great, some individuals react adversely to certain scents. For this reason, the source of the scent and the scent should be of right concentration and fresh to evoke the right smell. It is also necessary to ensure that the duration of the scent is within the usual range to elicit the right response.

ii) Spending time with animals

Studies indicate that pets can be beneficial to people with a variety of mental health issues such as anxiety. Pets offer love, companionship, and support. Most people prefer dogs, cats, and other small mammals as pets; people with allergies can find pets that do not have fur. In one study, caring for crickets was shown to enhance psychological health in older people. Investing time with animals can also lower anxiety and stress linked to trauma. In another study, grooming and spending time with horses can alleviate some of these effects.

iii)   Adequate sleep

Lack of good quality and adequate sleep causes inflammation and irritability. Several studies on the impact of sleep loss suggest that mediators of inflammation are altered by loss of sleep. For this reason, sleep loss will induce systemic and low-grade inflammation as well as irritability marked by the release of several molecules that include acute-phase proteins and cytokines.

Additionally, blood sugar imbalances are also caused by sleep deficiencies and enhanced cortisol secretion that aggravates inflammation increases with sleep deficiencies. These compounds are responsible for several health conditions, including diabetes, high blood pressure, and obesity. Having ideal adequate amounts of sleep lowers inflammation and restores the brain by taking out toxins. Beta-amyloid, which is a toxic protein accumulates in the brains of patients with Alzheimer's disease. Having adequate and quality sleep allows the neurological system to regulate appropriate neurotransmitters and replenish myelin sheaths that safeguard and shield nerve fibers.

Chapter 10: Be Kind to Yourself

Below are some of the things you can do to be kind to yourself. Some of these mentioned items are familiar, but a lot of them bear repeating.

1.   Cultivate awareness and set intentions

Self-awareness is one key to a successful self-relationship. Basically, knowing yourself will help you to know how you can relate to your own needs and fulfill your goals. Set your goals clearly, over days, weeks, and years, they will help you to build a relationship with yourself. Keep watch of the changes happening in your life.

2.   Plan plans for short, middle, and long-term

In the process of building a healthy relationship with self, it is important to set specific goals and priorities. Basically, life is about motivation, we go for what we want and feel good about getting it, and that builds our feelings for ourselves. For instance, if you join that class, you have always wanted to, you are likely to feel good and proud of yourself. The more we achieve things, the more we feel motivated to go for others. However, there is one challenge human being do not know how to deal with. You see, ones a person achieves something, he/she moves on quickly to others, thus chances of forgetting whatever we already know. By moving on, we forget how to maintain the habits and practices we have already started. A great general recipe for healthy self-relationship is to blend novelty with satisfaction in the long term. We often focus on short term gratification and forget about the long term rewards that become due in the future. So, have clear goals for both short term and long term.

3.   Adopt an attitude of acceptance and curiosity.

One reason why we fail to have an attitude of acceptance is that we fail to realize that change is inevitable. We try so much to control and maintain life in a specific way and fail to create room for change. It is important to embrace change, even when it stirs fear. Everyone is afraid of the unknown but how one handles fear determines success and consequently, self-relationship. In order to discover our true self, we need to go through different phases of life, change gradually, and finally discover our true purpose. Make changes when necessary and acknowledge that you cannot always control the outcome. If something does not feel right, avoid it, but if you are convinced to try out a new path, do it anyway. You might fail, but at least you will have tried. Be curious and go for what you want. The more you achieve, the more you will realize what you want.

4.   Prioritize your basic self-care

Eat well rest, sleep, pursue your passion and hobbies, and make yourself happy.   The simple mental habits you develop and follow on a daily basis are the foundation of your self-relationship. Sustainable self-care can be hard to achieve, and it will require a lot of basic dedication. Sometimes we are so busy building other things that we forget to care for ourselves. When was the last time you took yourself out for a movie or dinner without needing the company of another person? What about that massage?

Being in touch with your body and meeting its basic needs can be the first step towards a healthy self-relationship. It sounds so simple (taking care of our bodies) that we often ignore it, after all, it is something we have done since childhood. The advantage of taking care of oneself is that gradually, one begins to trust him/herself. Being a good custodian of that body shows others how they can treat you. And if others treat you nicely, it improves your self-relationship.

Habits are behaviors that have been practiced for so long that they become an automatic part of life. They can be hard to change, especially if we have practiced them for so long. In fact, there are some things we have done for so long that we actually think they are right, yet they are wrong. For instance, some of us are so used to skiving a meal (for instance, breakfast), and assuming that it has no effect. Here is the thing, such a habit has its effects. A good number of us have no idea how they can be happy by themselves, and they wonder how one can enjoy self-company.

5.   Be kind to yourself.

We always hear people say, be kind to yourself, be honest with yourself, be gentle with yourself, forgive yourself, et cetera. However, do we ever stop and appreciate the weight of such phrases? When was the last time you allowed yourself to make mistakes without judging yourself so harshly? Being kind to yourself does not mean letting yourself off the hook or avoiding responsibility. It means understanding that you are human and are prone to making mistakes. Therefore, self-kindness means appraising self without destructive self-blame and criticism. Human beings often find someone or something to blame or accuse, and more often than not, they use a destructive way to hold others responsible. Destructive self-criticism does not facilitate change. So, it is important to avoid self-blame and work towards gentle and kind.

6.   Seek other people who share your goal

On your quest to a better self-relationship, ensure that you surround yourself with people who have the same goals as you. If you keep the company of people who love themselves and appreciate their lives regardless of the situation, you will learn how to have a better self-relationship.   Having the right company will not only set a model for you but also offer the right support. It is impossible to avoid toxic people but as soon as you realize that a person is adding no value to your life, let them go or at least establish a healthy boundary.

7.   Cultivate optimistic and realistic behavior.

Sometimes, we set unrealistic goals for ourselves, and when we fail to achieve them, we feel incomplete or unaccomplished. Consequently, this affects our self-relationship. All or nothing mentality affects the relationship we have with ourselves. Perfectionism also drains so much energy from us, yet it is not always achievable. Most people try to fix everything in a very short time. That need always lead s to failure, negative thinking, a cycle of self-blame, and mental breakdown. In worse cases, perfectionism and an all or nothing spirit lead to more self-abuse and doubt. Those negative things are not helpful or a healthy self-relationship.

While many people insist that they have to set high self-standards in order to achieve their goals, it is not necessarily true. Being gentle to self can be of more benefits than practicing destructive perfectionism. It is better to learn from mistakes than beat yourself up because of failures. Many people practice maladaptive defenses because they want to experience changes in their lives. What they fail to realize is that building change gradually is better than expecting an instant makeover. For instance, instead of setting the goal of visiting the gym five times a week, two hours per session, one can start by going to the gym at least once a week. If he/she fails to meet these goals the first time, he/she can carry them over to the next day.

8.   Maintain meaningful activities.

Everyone wants to succeed, and we have different definitions of success. While often we concentrate on the best things to define success, the truth is, you are likely to get more satisfaction in life if you do things that give you a sense of accomplishment. Not everyone has their dream job, yet they have to work to get their income. While working in an environment that you do not like, find a way to make it interesting and satisfactory. You do not change what you do; maybe all it takes to feel accomplished is to change how you work. It is also important to maintain relationships that mean something to you. Ensure that you engage in activities outside the norm, such as recreation activities, hobbies, voluntary works, et cetera. Your mind is a great source of satisfaction if you know what to focus on.

Another study conducted by Harvard psychologist Dr. Matt Killingsworth reveals that humans are far less happy when they are daydreaming. Focusing on worries about the future can easily rob you the gift of the present. It could prevent you from actually doing something to improve your situation. Time is important and while daydreaming is not always a bad thing, spending too much time on it is not a good idea. That time could have been spent with family or friends. Spending too much time away from the present is not a good way to experience life.

It will take time and effort to teach our minds not to daydream too much, but it is doable. Here are some pointers you can follow:

Practice Mindfulness

You don't need to be a monk who is adept at meditation to practice the art of mindfulness. Try the mindfulness exercises in chapter 13.

You can practice the simple joy of being conscious and aware by making the effort to eat your breakfast without any form of distraction. Feel the warmth of coffee in your mouth, savor the bittersweet taste and smell the aroma of the wonderful drink. Try to use your five senses and what you can gain from the present. Try to do this as regularly as you can, but for starters, you can begin with a simple activity that you regularly do every day.

Regain the Focus on the Simplicity of Life

As soon as you notice that your mind is wandering off again, immediately regain your focus. Get your attention back to something that is simple and monotonous right at the moment. It could be a piece of paper, a paper bill, a cup of coffee, a notebook, or even just your hand.

Try to focus on things that will not trigger any emotion. The goal is to concentrate all of your attention on the item that will bring your awareness back to the present. You can do this each time you find yourself daydreaming until you are ready to naturally move on to what it is that you are actually doing.

Do New Things Every Day

Have you realized that when we were kids, the day seemed to pass by slowly? This is partly because when we were kids, we are experiencing life for the first time, and processing it all requires our complete attention. It is ideal to focus our attention when we try new things and notice how much of the attention we manage to win over. We have to focus so we can learn how to do something. We generally have to steer ourselves to the present as we do or learn to do new things.

Acceptance

Acceptance is considered as an alternative approach for experiential avoidance. It also involves the conscious and active acceptance of personal history without trying to change its form or frequency, especially if doing so will result in damage to the person's psychological health.

For instance, people who are suffering from anxiety are encouraged to feel anxiety as an emotion that is natural for people to feel. Meanwhile, people who are suffering from chronic pain are encouraged to undergo specific treatments that will allow them to cope. Take note that this process is not an end in itself. Instead, it is developed as a way to increase actions that are based on values.

Most people who are suffering from anxiety usually find it odd when they are advised by their ACT specialists to accept something that has been causing them suffering. This may not make sense initially. Some people ask "Why would we want to accept anxiety? Doesn't that mean that we have to live with this harmful emotion?"

But that's the ACT way. The process requires acceptance, after which you will have to go. It may sound contradictory because how can you let go of something that you have already accepted?

Keep in mind that language is used to represent something, and that there are instances when they also represent what is beyond the literal meaning. In the most literal sense, acceptance refers to the action of receiving something.

Old school mental health practitioners have promoted the idea of acceptance as learning how to live with something, and in this example, anxiety. However, this notion could be detrimental as it may build an internal conflict that can cause confusion and can even make the anxiety worse.

Conclusion

Thank you for making it through to the end Cognitive Behavioral Therapy: *The 10 steps CBT workbook with techniques for retraining your brain made simple. For managing anxiety, depression, anger, panic and intrusive thoughts.* The author ensured that the CBT workbook covers all essential techniques for retraining your brain to get rid of anxiety, depression, anger, panic, and other negative conditions.

I hope you have learned a lot about different forms and techniques of behavioral therapy, and you are now better armed to reshape your life. By now, you should have a better understanding of the possible treatment program you want to try.

Let us hope it was educative and able to provide you with all of the tools you need to achieve your goals, whatever it is that they may be. Just because you've finished this book doesn't mean there is nothing left to learn on the topic, expanding your horizons is the only way to find the mastery you seek.

You have the power to make yourself feel better, through working on cognitive and behavioral interventions. You can learn to deal with anything that faces you. If you work on using these skills diligently and find that you still need help, seek out at a therapist that is trained in CBT to help you. Sometimes an outside perspective or voice is necessary to help you get the perspective you need on what is going on in your own mind.

Always remember that if you feel that you are in danger of hurting yourself, you have to reach out. There are many people that can help you. Look into the suicide hotline in your country or reach out to emergency services. There is always a chance for your life to get better, remember that.

Finally, if you found this book useful in any way, a review on Amazon is always appreciated!

www.ingramcontent.com/pod-product-compliance
Lightning Source LLC
Chambersburg PA
CBHW061812250726

48657CB00001B/404